Contents

Home Secretary Foreword

Preventing, reducing and detecting crime; providing safety and security for law-abiding citizens and their families – this is what effective policing is about and it is at the heart of civil society. We owe the men and women of our police service a tremendous debt of gratitude for the challenging and sometimes dangerous job that they do. We also owe them our help and support to enable them to deliver effective policing. This is why we have embarked on an ambitious and far-reaching programme of reform.

Working closely with the service, we have seen tangible development and achievements. There are record police officer numbers and 4,000 community support officers. Crime has fallen by 30% since 1997. We are cutting bureaucracy and making wider, better use of new technology and scientific techniques. We have embedded effective performance management throughout the service. Fear of crime is falling. Through more effective partnership working, use of new powers and best practice, we are getting a grip on anti-social behaviour. The chances of being a victim of crime are at the lowest level for over 20 years.

This paper sets out a clear direction of change as we move into the second phase of reform – to deliver community policing for today's world and face the new challenges of changing criminality.

We will spread dedicated neighbourhood policing teams across the country. They will be supported by continued substantial investment that will maintain officer numbers and provide 25,000 community support officers and wardens.

We will embed a genuinely responsive customer-service culture and make the police and their partners more accessible, visible and accountable.

A new improvement agency will ensure that policing is driven by intelligence, good practice and performance information.

We will modernise the police workforce, enhancing training and career progression to improve leadership and management skills at all levels of the service. Continuing to cut bureaucracy will free up the equivalent of 12,000 officers to front-line policing by 2008.

We will professionalise the critical role of the police constable as the lynchpin of neighbourhood policing teams. Reform will be at all levels of policing and criminality – from the very local, through regional and cross-border co-operation, to the strategic force and national level.

Working with the service and communities, this Government is committed to a broad and ambitious programme of change to shape the future of policing. We are clear that this is reform for a purpose. It is reform that builds upon and enhances the core role of the police to reduce crime and anti-social behaviour. It is reform to reinforce respect for the law and to protect and empower law-abiding citizens and communities. We are not imposing reform. We are working collaboratively to set the national framework within which forces, police authorities, local government and local people can work together to build safer and more secure communities.

David Blunkett

Rt Hon David Blunkett MP
Home Secretary

Executive Summary

Context

The world in which the police service operates today has changed beyond all recognition. Technology has removed borders and barriers; changes in society have opened up new opportunities and challenges; increasing investment in public services and a growing consumer culture has led to rising expectations of customer service. The core role of the police service is, and will remain, prevention, detection and reduction of crime, and protecting the public. The Government is already helping the police to perform this role more effectively through investment in new technology, greater use of forensics and better gathering, management and use of intelligence in policing.

Like all public services, the police service cannot be immune from further change and continuous improvement. Indeed the service has shown itself prepared and willing to embrace change and meet new challenges, whilst maintaining the enduring values of the British police.

Sustained reform and investment

The Government and the police service are already engaged in a sustained programme of investment and reform that has achieved real results:

- record police officer numbers of nearly 140,000 – up 13,000 on 1997 and 39,000 more than 30 years ago;

- introduction of 4,000 community support officers with a commitment to recruiting 25,000 CSOs and wardens by 2008;

- improvements in scientific and technological support; and

- a sustained focus on police performance.

This police commitment and Government investment have led to a drop in overall crime by 30% since 1997. The chances of being a victim of crime are at their lowest levels since the British Crime Survey began in 1981.

This paper sets out the Government's vision for continued improvements in policing to help build safety, security and stability in our communities. We want to continue to reduce crime, to tackle anti-social behaviour and disorder, to reduce people's fear of crime and to ensure that law-abiding citizens, families and their children are protected.

Objectives

Underpinning the clear requirement that the primary job of the police is to prevent, deter, detect and reduce crime, this paper has three broad objectives at its heart:

- the first is the spread of neighbourhood policing for the 21st century to every community with improved police responsiveness and customer service;

- the second is further modernisation of the police workforce to ensure that the service is fully equipped and able to deliver these changes;

- the third is the greater involvement of communities and citizens in determining how their communities are policed.

Bureaucracy

A critical element of delivering a more visible and accessible police service is the Government and police service's continuing drive to reduce bureaucracy and free up more officers for front-line policing. We are removing unnecessary burdens, scrapping unnecessary forms, offering practical assistance to forces through the appointment of an assistant chief constable who is visiting forces to spread good practice and the introduction of an actionline. By 2008 – by cutting bureaucracy, improving science and technological support, and other reforms – we will have freed up the equivalent of 12,000 officers for front-line duties.

Revitalised community policing for today's world

Revitalised neighbourhood and community policing for the 21st century is central to the Government's approach. By 2008 we want every community to benefit from the level and style of neighbourhood policing that they need. This will involve dedicated teams of police officers, community support officers and wardens providing a visible, reassuring presence, preventing and detecting crime and developing a constructive and lasting engagement with members of their community.

Neighbourhood policing teams

Fully trained officers using modern techniques and updated powers, working with CSOs with a minimum set of powers, will make up neighbourhood policing teams. They will take an intelligence-led, proactive, problem-solving approach to enable them to focus on and tackle specific local issues. They will involve their local community in establishing and negotiating priorities for action and in identifying and implementing solutions. They will ensure a two-way flow of information with the community to build trust and co-operation to help them deal more effectively with crime and anti-social behaviour. Police and their partners providing useful and meaningful information on how a community is being policed will encourage and empower individuals to work with the police, feeding community intelligence into crime prevention, detection and reduction. This is not a substitute for, rather an underpinning of, solid, professional police work to investigate crime and catch criminals – necessary to tackle systematic and organised criminality.

£50 million of new money for the Neighbourhood Policing Fund will deliver 2,000 community support officers during the course of this financial year. Many forces are already putting in place successful and effective neighbourhood policing. We will build on this good practice by providing support for 25,000 community support officers and wardens by 2008.

Responsiveness

Neighbourhood policing is at its most effective when it is a shared undertaking with the local community. People, and in particular victims and witnesses, will only engage with their local police if they have confidence that when they make contact they will be treated well and that their concerns will be listened to and acted on effectively.

Instilling a strong customer service culture throughout the police service is therefore a central objective of the reforms set out in this paper.

Minimum national standards

Forces, Basic Command Units and neighbourhood teams will deliver services with the needs of their users very firmly in mind. They will act on customer feedback to generate continuous improvement in the service they provide. This means delivering guaranteed standards of customer service to the public whenever they have contact with the police. Every force will have these standards in place within two years and will agree with their communities how the standards can be built on locally.

As a result of these changes it will be far easier to contact the police; the way calls from the public are handled will be improved; and victims will be better informed on the progress of their cases. In addition to improving the general information to the public about the availability of services we also intend to put in place a national non-emergency number, linking into a range of services, to improve the effectiveness of dealing with non-emergency calls. Performance measurement of the police will include a level of public satisfaction.

What will be different?

People will see a more visible, accessible police presence on the streets and in their communities – making full use of the record numbers of officers in the service. There will be clearer and easier means of contacting the police and other services to deal with problems. The service provided will be professional, courteous and will be designed to meet people's diverse needs and give them maximum confidence that their problems and concerns will be dealt with.

For example, if you have an anti-social behaviour problem in your street – persistent graffiti or vandalism – then you will be able to discuss this with your local neighbourhood officer or community support officer. You will know who that person is or, if you don't, you will very quickly and easily be able to find out how best to make contact with them. If you are not sure who the right person to contact is you will be able to use the single, national non-emergency number that we will introduce. However you make contact and whoever you make contact with, you can be clear of the standard and quality of service that you are entitled to receive. Your local officers will work with you and your neighbours to identify the most appropriate solution to the problem and work together with their partners in the local authority or other local agencies and communities themselves to deliver that solution.

A dynamic, modern workforce

Developing a modern police workforce is essential as the foundation for delivering successfully the changes that we describe in this paper – as well as continuing to drive down crime and provide safety and security. We need to foster and build a culture of learning and self-improvement within the police service. It has to be a service in which the contribution of everyone – officers, police staff and volunteers – is fully recognised and used to the full in the delivery of front line services.

Leadership at all levels

The role of the police officer is, and will remain, fundamental to the success of the police service. Constables are taking on increasingly skilled roles within neighbourhood policing teams, managing a diverse range of staff and acting as community leaders. We want to help them to do that. We will work with the police service to equip leaders at all levels of the service with the knowledge, skills, confidence and freedom they need to do this.

Sergeants and inspectors will have access to training to develop their managerial, leadership and operational skills. Over time there will be a mandatory qualification for superintendents seeking to become Basic Command Unit commanders.

Career development

Measures in this paper build on work already in hand to develop an integrated approach to career development in the police service. The foundations of this approach are national occupational standards and an effective Performance and Development Review system. We will introduce proper career development for all members at every level of the service. We will remove barriers to entry at levels above constable and we will end time limits on promotion. We will remove barriers for police staff becoming police officers, and enhance the skills and roles of police staff.

Powers

We will strengthen the roles of police staff and introduce national standards and a minimum set of powers for community support officers. These minimum powers will contribute towards freeing up police officers for frontline policing by including the power to issue a range of fixed penalty notices. Following a successful pilot in six forces, we will empower all forces to be able to give their CSOs the power of detention. We are also committed to ensuring that the powers available to police officers themselves are up-to-date and effective – equipping them for the difficult and demanding range of tasks that we call on the police to perform.

Equality

The Government and the police service remain firmly committed to race and gender equality. We are putting forward measures to increase the rates of recruitment, retention and progression of minority ethnic, female and other under-represented groups in the service.

What will be different?

A modernised police workforce will support our drive towards a service which is focused relentlessly on the needs of the law-abiding citizen.

You, the citizen, will continue to see a much greater police presence in your community as a result of the growth in the workforce and the more effective deployment of officers, CSOs and police staff. The service will reflect the community in which you live in terms of its diversity of background, experience, skills and knowledge.

You, the police officer, CSO, or police staff member will benefit from our commitment to skills development and career progression. You will have improved opportunities and a clearer career pathway through the service. Reduced bureaucracy and improved powers will mean that you are better able to do the job that you want to do, that you were trained to do and that your community expects you to do.

Greater involvement of communities and citizens

To be more responsive and citizen-focused and be successful at reducing crime, the police service must be much more closely engaged with local people.

Information

Local people need to be clear who is responsible for what in terms of community safety. They need to understand how they as individuals, families and members of the community, can play a role in keeping their communities safe and in preventing and reducing crime; how they can have a say in setting local priorities, and how well their local police are performing. This information needs to be available to every household and people should know what they can do, including how to trigger action through their local councillor, if local problems are not being tackled effectively.

Community advocacy

We want to enhance the current role of councillors and local authority community safety officers to give them an explicit remit to provide a focal point for the local community in terms of dealing with those agencies responsible for community safety. They would ensure effective representation of people's concerns and empower people to work with the police and others to find better solutions to their problems. They would ensure that local people's views are represented on the quality of service provided by the police and other community safety agencies.

Triggering action

If the service that a community receives does not meet the standards set out in their local contract with the police, or if there is a particular problem associated with crime or anti-social behaviour, there will be a specific mechanism to trigger action at a number of different levels. At the first level, this will be to gain information that is not already available. At the next, it will be to require attendance by the police or relevant local agency at a public meeting to discuss the issues and explain what action they are going to take. It could also lead to a specific request to take certain actions to address the problem. If the agencies decided that no action was to be taken, the agencies concerned would need to explain why.

Police and local authorities

The changes set out in this paper cannot be achieved by focusing solely on local communities and neighbourhoods, nor can a sustained reduction in crime and anti-social behaviour. The local government cabinet member with responsibility for community safety will sit on the police authority to strengthen democratic accountability. The role of police authorities in ensuring effective delivery of policing will also be strengthened. They will oversee local consultation, including the relationship between Crime and Disorder Reduction Partnerships and neighbourhood bodies. We will also enhance their role in holding chief officers to account.

Local to national

Nor can neighbourhood policing, vitally important though it is, be looked at in isolation. Unless the police are effective at tackling crime and criminality from the local to the national level, then the public will not have confidence that the service is actually delivering. Alongside proposals in relation to responsiveness and customer service we also need to strengthen the service as a whole. This means effective leaders at every level within the police service, working with strengthened partnerships; better approaches to tackling cross-border and serious organised crime; national coherence on issues such as the gathering, management and sharing of intelligence; effective use of science and technological advances; robust performance management arrangements; and a National Intelligence Model effectively used by all forces.

What will be different?

The police service will be more accountable to local democratic structures and to their local community. Police authorities will be more closely connected with and visible to their local community so that the line of accountability is clear.

You will be kept fully informed about policing in your local area – performance as well as who is responsible for what. You will know who to go to and how to contact them when you have concerns or problems relating to delivery of community safety services in your areas. Most importantly, you will know where to go if you are dissatisfied and need redress for the service you have received. In extreme cases, you will be able to trigger action to address your concerns.

We have a great deal for which to be grateful to the men and women of the police service – for their integrity, their effort, their concern for their fellow citizens and for their courage. This policy paper is aimed at enabling them to deliver, in the future, an even more effective service to the communities they serve.

Chapter One: Building a better police service

Chapter One: Building a better police service

This chapter summarises the Government's approach to further reform of policing in England and Wales; what it wants to achieve; what it believes the core role and responsibilities of the police service should be; and what reform will mean for the citizen, for the police service itself and for those working with and within it.

Introduction

1.1 Effective policing is at the heart of civil society. It provides safety and security for law-abiding citizens and families, protects them from crime and anti-social behaviour and encourages stability in our communities. In all these respects, our country has been indebted to its police service for over 175 years, since Robert Peel introduced the concept of a professional service with the police officer as the citizen in uniform – thus laying the foundation of the police service of today.

1.2 These fundamental concepts endure. Many of the essential requirements of the police service – absolute and total integrity, courage, concern for all within society and service to the citizen – remain just as crucial today as they did 175 years ago. But there are real and considerable pressures for change. The public today has higher expectations; society is more open; family and community relationships have changed; we have instant global communications; crime and criminality continually reinvent themselves and the threats to the law-abiding citizen and to civil society change and grow. The police service can and must itself change and grow to meet the challenges of today's world.

1.3 The police service itself recognises that further changes and improvements are needed. The Government's continuing commitment to working with the police service and supporting this process – to build a better police service for the 21st Century – is total. It is Government's role to set the national direction, strategic framework and targets for policing in this country. This policy paper stands as part of that process. But within this overall framework – part of which is about encouraging a new dynamic in terms of the involvement and engagement of the public in building safer communities – the Government is clear that locally, it is for chief constables and police authorities to deliver effective, responsive policing to the communities they serve.

1.4 The main thrust of our reforms is to pass power from the political centre to local citizens and communities, to create new democratic accountabilities and scrutiny, and to reinforce the role of elected councillors in local policing. This policy paper establishes a broad framework of local control and accountability, but local people will have the common sense and ingenuity to devise workable local arrangements appropriate to their circumstances. Our communities are diverse, and effective local policing must reflect local differences.

Reform does not begin here

1.5 This paper sets out an ambitious agenda for change which represents the next stage in the necessary evolution of policing to help ensure safety, security and stability in communities across England and Wales. But reform does not begin and end here. This is a developing agenda which builds on the sustained programme of reform, which has been taken forward by the police service and the Government together, and the progress that has already been made in terms of making policing in this country more effective. Real results continue to be achieved across the country through the hard work of police forces, police authorities and their local and national partners.

1.6 We now have more police officers (at nearly 140,000) and police staff (at over 67,000) in this country than ever before, together with over 4,000 new community support officers. Police officers are better paid and supported – police pay has increased by 26% in real terms since 1997. We have increased London allowances for officers by £3,000; introduced a new South East allowance; increased paternity leave and introduced adoption leave and provision for time off to care for dependents.

1.7 Despite this substantial growth in police numbers, people have the perception that there are fewer police on the streets. We are therefore engaged in a major drive to get the police out of their stations, out of their cars and back into communities – to provide the more visible, accessible service that the public wants to see. This is vital for increasing trust and confidence in policing. With the growing civiliansation of particular roles, improved technical support like video identification parades, the introduction of Fixed Penalty Notices for disorder and the removal of unnecessary paperwork, we are freeing up more officers for the frontline. Twenty years ago, legal challenges and the erosion of public confidence led the Government of the day to bring in the Police and

Criminal Evidence Act (PACE). Whilst retaining the important protection contained in that Act, we have revised its accompanying procedures to reduce bureaucracy. We have, and will continue to modernise other powers to ensure that the entire police workforce can operate as effectively as possible in tackling crime.

1.8 Led in many cases by the police service itself, we have seen the introduction of the new Airwave police radio communications system and the development of a world-leading DNA database. We have seen a real focus on police performance and intelligence-led policing starting to take hold within forces. But recognising that the police cannot be responsible for delivering safer communities on their own, we have also recognised the importance of effective partnership working. The bodies we have established such as Crime and Disorder Reduction Partnerships and Local Criminal Justice Boards are vital elements in our approach. This progress has been underpinned by sustained Government investment in police funding – which has increased by 21% in real terms since 1997. And the results of all this are that the chances of being a victim of crime are now at historically low levels and the number of burglaries, robberies and vehicle crimes – the so-called volume crimes – have all fallen sharply. We explore this progress further in Chapter Two of this paper along with the pressures for further change.

1.9 Most recently, the Government set out proposals for further reform of policing in its consultation paper in November 2003[1] – to which there was a substantial and constructive response.[2] This has helped inform the proposals in this paper – as

---

[1] *Policing: Building Safer Communities Together* – published 4 November 2003, available at www.policereform.gov.uk

[2] Published on 9 September 2004, available at www.policereform.gov.uk

have other thoughtful views from a range of stakeholders both within and outside the police service; by best practice examples from around the country and by a growing body of evidence of what works in terms of reducing crime, bringing offenders to justice and reassuring communities. Fundamentally, the approach outlined in this paper reflects what the Government believes the public wants to see from its police service.

1.10 The Government is at one with the leadership of the police service in England and Wales about the need for – and importantly – the direction of change. It is the ability of the police service in this country to embrace change, and get things done, that makes the Government confident about making further improvements for the benefit of all our communities.

> "We believe that reform at intervals is insufficient and that 'constant transformation' is the only approach to serve the public well in the 21st century… we believe that we are the guardians of the service we offer, not of the structure we inhabit."
>
> (From the Association of Chief Police Officers' response to *Policing: Building Safer Communities Together*)

What do we want to achieve?

1.11 The Government's goal is, quite simply, to make policing better – to help build safety, security and stability in communities across England and Wales. We want to further reduce crime and anti-social behaviour; reduce people's fear of crime and anti-social behaviour; and ensure that law-abiding citizens and families are protected. We believe that the police also play an important role in rebuilding respect in our communities. But we recognise that the police cannot do everything themselves – effective partnership working is vital.

1.12 We want to improve the performance of all police forces in England and Wales with forces doing better, with partners, at preventing, investigating and detecting crime and bringing more offenders to justice. And we want this to be combined with high levels of public satisfaction, trust and confidence in the police, particularly amongst victims of crime and ethnic minority communities. But we cannot do this from the centre. With operational responsibility at the local level, it must be the job of the leaders of each force and police authority to ensure that this happens.

1.13 Fundamentally, the Government wants to ensure that the police service in England and Wales is, and is seen by its workforce and the public, to be a genuine *service*, not simply a collection of disparate police forces.

The police service has the key role in keeping communities safe…

1.14 There are certain constants in terms of the role which the police service has in our history and society. This role is founded on core values which the Government believes should not change – the police being independent and non-political; demonstrating a commitment to public service not social control; with officers and staff enforcing the law, keeping the peace and acting with absolute integrity at all times. And the police, like everyone else, are accountable to the law. On its establishment 175 years ago, the role of the Metropolitan Police was defined as:

> "The prevention of crime… the protection of life and property, the preservation of public tranquility."[3]

---

[3] From Sir Richard Mayne's instructions to the 'New Police of the Metropolis', 1829.

1.15 A number of reports, academic studies and (in Scotland at least) Acts of Parliament[4] have sought to encapsulate the core role of the police in Britain. The Scarman Report in 1981 for example, following the unrest in Brixton in April that year, took the description quoted above as the authoritative definition of the role of the police (and asserted that, if necessary, the "maintenance of public tranquility comes first").[5]

1.16 Policing does not, of course, exist in a time capsule. It is the product of history, local circumstance, political and societal changes and, in some senses, compromise. As the 1962 Royal Commission on the Police asserted for example:

> "…the police should be powerful but not oppressive; they should be efficient but not officious…".[6]

1.17 Since the 1962 Royal Commission, a number of Reports and Inquiries have had a bearing on the role which the police play in our country. For

example, the 1977 Committee of Inquiry on the Police under Lord Edmund-Davies focused on the pay and conditions of officers to ensure the service attracted and retained the best people to perform what was seen as an expanding role. Other reports have been significant – the 1981 Scarman Report mentioned above for example; the report of the Taylor Inquiry into the Hillsborough disaster; the Macpherson Report of the Stephen Lawrence Inquiry; Lord Laming's Report into the death of Victoria Climbie; and most recently Sir Michael Bichard's Report following the Soham murders have, along with the findings contained in other reports, influenced and led more directly to changes in the way policing in this country is done and the role which the police service itself plays in our society. Our proposals for the future of policing have been framed in the context of a rapidly changing economic, social and cultural environment. They respond to the changing needs of people themselves; changed behaviour; changing forms of criminality and the need to reinforce and rebuild respect, decency, self-restraint and care for others.

1.18 So the duties of the police – and the emphasis that is placed upon them – change as society changes, from generation to generation. There are some functions which, over time, have now largely become the responsibility of others – the protection of animals and the routine protection of commercial property for example. Other functions have been added, even relatively recently, such as the statutory involvement in

---

[4] The Police (Scotland) Act 1967 defines the general functions and jurisdiction of constables which have been interpreted as describing the function of the police in general. These functions include a duty to "guard, patrol and watch so as to prevent the commission of offences, preserve order and to protect life and property" (Chapter 77, Part I, s.17 of the Police (Scotland) act 1967 refers).

[5] The Brixton Disorders 10-12 April 1981: Report of an Inquiry by the Rt. Hon. The Lord Scarman, OBE – November 1981 (Cmnd 8427).

[6] Royal Commission on the Police 1962 (Cmnd 1728) – paragraph 57.

partnership working to reduce crime and disorder in communities as required by the Crime and Disorder Act 1998.

1.19 The challenges facing policing today are huge – in scale and complexity. So it is important, in proposing changes to meet those challenges, that we explore what the role of the police service should be for this generation. In doing so, the Government recognises that the police service in England and Wales has already accumulated over time a broad role which goes far beyond that requiring formal police powers.

1.20 But the Government takes as its starting point the core duties of the constable, who is required by legislation to affirm to serve the crown:

"…with fairness, integrity, diligence and impartiality, upholding fundamental human rights and according equal respect to all people; and that I will, to the best of my power, cause the peace to be kept and preserved and prevent all offences against people and property; and that while I continue to hold the said office I will, to the best of my skill and knowledge, discharge all the duties thereof faithfully according to the law."[7]

1.21 The Government's clear view is that the police service in England and Wales must have a broad role, based in part on the core elements set out in the attestation for constables set out above. We believe this is vital in terms of maintaining the legitimacy of the police service in the eyes of the public and meeting our desire to see increased trust and confidence in policing in this country.

1.22 The Government believes that policing in today's world needs to be about both preventing and detecting crime and reassuring the public. Our view is that excellent forces can and should do both, as should police officers themselves. Visible interaction with the public provides reassurance but also vital intelligence to help arrest criminals and tackle all levels of crime – from anti-social behaviour to serious organised crime and terrorism; tackling crime effectively delivers, in turn, reassurance to local communities.

1.23 Policing is, clearly, not an exact science. Indeed it is an increasingly complex and challenging activity. Within the kind of broad role outlined above, the Government recognises that police forces perform complex and interlocking functions – and that these operate from the very local to the national level and beyond. There will always be a need for the police to act as the service of last resort – to protect life, respond to emergencies and manage crises – and be able to do so for 24 hours of the day; 365 days of the year. So forces will have to maintain a reactive capability to respond to incidents in real time.

1.24 But the Government's view is that the policing pendulum has swung too far in the reactive direction. We believe there needs to be a shift towards more proactive, problem-solving policing – with forces getting better at preventing crime

7 Schedule 4 to the Police Act 1996 as amended by section 83 of the Police Reform Act 2002.

happening in the first place, but also being better at solving it when it does happen. It was no accident of drafting that the first function ascribed to the then new Metropolitan Police in 1829 was to *prevent* crime. We believe that policing has shifted too far away from this ideal. So we place particular emphasis – as has the police service itself in recent years – on the need to embed a truly problem-solving, intelligence-led approach to policing throughout forces in England and Wales. This is behind the emphasis in this paper on dedicated neighbourhood policing for today's world, not that of the 19th century; increasing the responsiveness and customer service of the police; engaging better with the public and further modernising the police workforce – equipping police officers and police staff with the skills to meet the challenges of 21st century policing.

1.25 The Government wants to see a police service with the capability to deliver the breadth of its role – protecting individuals, securing public safety, preventing and reducing crime, bringing criminals to justice, working with children, young people and families – including safeguarding them from harm – reassuring the public and helping to build strong, cohesive communities. The Government believes that the proposals in this policy paper will enable and empower the police service to fulfill these responsibilities.

...but keeping communities safe is not just a job for the police

1.26 Although the police service plays now – and will continue to play – the key role in reducing crime and anti-social behaviour and ensuring community safety, the Government is clear that these are not matters for which the service alone is responsible. Effective partnership work involving other criminal justice agencies, local government and health agencies, children's services and the voluntary and business sectors is vital. And the police need to work with national agencies like the National Crime Squad, the National Criminal Intelligence Service (which will shortly be subsumed into the new serious Organised Crime Agency that we discuss in Chapter Five) and our security and intelligence services to tackle serious organised crime and terrorism.

1.27 The Government is similarly clear in its belief that individuals and communities themselves have a role in this partnership. Local policing, for example, is at its most effective when performed as a shared undertaking: policing being done with the public. This is about individuals recognising their own responsibilities in terms of helping to prevent and reduce crime, not just their right to live in safer communities.

1.28 The Government is clear about the role it can and should play – in setting the national direction and strategic framework within which local policing should be delivered and providing resources and powers to tackle crime and anti-social behaviour. The Government also believes it has a role in establishing priorities in order to ensure safety and security across our communities and for our nation; offering support to police forces where this is needed but protecting the public by intervening in cases of demonstrable failure or where, in the national interest, coherence in policing practices is required. The Government also has a clear role in helping build confidence and enabling and empowering people to play a real and active part in keeping their own neighbourhoods and communities safe. The Government recognises the need itself to be better joined up at a national level in terms of community safety issues.

1.29 The success of the approach to policing outlined in this paper therefore depends, in part, on the support and work of others – local authorities, for example, exercising their responsibility for community safety; effective partnership work happening everywhere; more being done through education and social services to prevent young people becoming involved in crime; the whole criminal justice system working together more coherently to catch, convict and rehabilitate offenders; and probation, employment and health services working to resettle offenders and address drugs misuse. Overall, we believe in an approach which strikes a balance between help and support for individuals and families who need it – and tough enforcement for those who break the law.

1.30 This paper should also be seen in the context of wider work taking place to build security in our country and which puts the law-abiding citizen first – such as that detailed in the Home Office and Criminal Justice five year Strategic Plans published in July 2004.[8] And, whilst recognising that some elements of policing differ from other services, the Government's wider public service reform agenda also provides an important context. Further details of key elements of this can be found in Appendix I to this paper.

What does this mean for the future direction of policing?

Neighbourhood policing

1.31 The Government believes that, as a starting point, we need revitalised neighbourhood policing for today's world. Our clear view is that increasing public trust and confidence in policing – while important in its own right – will also be a real benefit for the police service itself. It will help make policing more effective. We believe this requires the spread of dedicated neighbourhood policing teams across the country to provide a visible, uniformed, accessible presence for the public. Our continued drive to reduce

unnecessary bureaucracy, civilianise posts and improve the technical support for policing will see more officers on the frontline. We see police officers continuing to be the lynchpin in neighbourhood teams – but with those officers working increasingly with police staff, community support officers (CSOs) and wardens using intelligence and real-time data to focus resources and respond to changing needs, backed up by the latest technology. Our Neighbourhood Policing Fund will support and drive this approach. We will deliver 25,000 CSOs and wardens by 2008.

Responsiveness, customer service and community engagement

1.32 The Government will seek to improve markedly the responsiveness and customer service culture of the police – including the treatment and support given to victims and witnesses. The first contact people have with the police – wherever that takes place – is crucial in determining people's perception of and confidence in policing. It is an area where we and the police service itself believe there is a clear and pressing need for improvement. And this underpins our approach to neighbourhood policing which, at this very local level, is at its most effective when performed as a shared undertaking with the public. This means moving from traditional notions of policing simply by consent or people's passive acquiescence, to policing with the proactive engagement and co-operation of communities. But if people are to engage, they need to be confident that they will be treated well, and their voices heard and acted upon.

1.33 The detail of how the Government intends to embed dedicated neighbourhood policing across the country and a new culture of responsiveness and customer service within the police service is

---

[8] *Confident Communities in a Secure Britain* (Cm 6287) and *Cutting Crime, Delivering Justice* (Cm 6288).

set out in Chapter Three of this paper. But there are some other important changes, set out below, which are vital to achieving the objectives of our programme for change and improvement. We see all the elements as being inextricably linked.

A new police workforce

1.34 The Government will continue to develop a more modernised police workforce since, ultimately, it is people – not structures or mechanisms – who are going to deliver the kind of truly responsive police service which has the trust and confidence of communities – to which we aspire and the public wants to see.

1.35 Our approach means building a workforce which is more representative of the communities it serves; is more unified, more flexible and has a better mix of skills. We want to see a service where police officers, police staff and volunteers feel truly valued and get the support they deserve; operate with professionalism, honesty and integrity at all times; and are properly recognised and rewarded for the jobs they do. And this means having quality training, learning, effective leadership and management at all levels – including, crucially, at the level of the police constable – and a continued emphasis on reducing unnecessary bureaucracy and increasing efficiency. Our aim is for a police service which encourages innovation, is more open and self-challenging and demonstrates a thirst for continuous self-improvement. We believe these changes are vital if we are to embed a true customer service culture within the police service. We set out our proposals for modernising the police workforce in Chapter Four of this paper.

Effective policing from local to national level

1.36 Though vitally important in its own right, the Government does not see neighbourhood policing taking place in isolation from policing at other levels. The effects of organised crime, like drugs smuggling at a national level for example,

all too readily manifest themselves on our streets and estates. We, and the police service, cannot hope to build the kind of deeper engagement with the public leading to increased trust and confidence in policing – if crime is not tackled effectively at every level.

1.37 Building on the spread of neighbourhood policing teams, this means having empowered police leaders at Basic Command Unit level together with strengthened partnership arrangements to reduce crime; tackling cross border crime; increased cooperation and collaboration at police force level and improved arrangements for tackling serious organised crime and terrorism. It means having national consistency about certain elements of policing like the collection and sharing of intelligence. And it means policing as a whole being supported by continued scientific and technological advances, modernised powers and systematic use of the National Intelligence Model as the core way of doing operational police business. We look at these issues in Chapter Five of this paper.

Clearer, stronger methods for ensuring effective policing

1.38 Again, underpinning our approach to increasing the responsiveness of, and community engagement in, policing, the Government believes that people need to be clear about who is responsible for what in terms of keeping their communities safe – and how they themselves can play a part and have a say in what their local priorities for policing should be. The public should know how well those with responsibility are performing – and how they can be held to account. For the public, how the present so-called tripartite arrangement for policing between the Home Secretary, chief constables and police authorities works is, at best, opaque. Clarifying and strengthening the existing arrangements are vital in terms of increasing trust and confidence in policing in this country. Chapter Five sets out our proposals for change to the present arrangements.

Our Vision for Neighbourhood Policing

Focused throughout by:

– ten commitments to citizens

– ten commitments to frontline officers

– the National Intelligence Model

The Citizen

A responsive neighbourhood policing team
(Officers, CSOs, wardens, specials, volunteers)

Supported by wider partnerships to cut crime
(led by BCU commanders with local government, voluntary sector, CJS agencies and others)

Driven by strong police leadership and accountability
(Chief Constables and Police Authorities)

Within a framework of national support
(National Policing Improvement Agency, SOCA, National Policing Plan)

What will reform mean to local people?

1.39 The Government is clear that the public needs to see and feel improvements if our reform programme is to succeed. In terms of the vision for further change set out in this paper, we think that citizens should see improvements in a number of key respects – set out in the 10 Commitments below.

10 Commitments to the public

The Government believes that **citizens** should:

1. be and feel safer in their homes and communities;

2. know who their local police officer, community support officer and wardens are – and who is in charge locally – and how they can be contacted; and receive relevant information about what is being done to tackle crime and keep their community safe;

3. receive a much better service when they contact the police; be confident about getting help quickly in an emergency and receive a better service from the police and other agencies in dealing with calls about important but non-emergency issues;

4. be clear about the level of service they can expect from their local police; understand that the police cannot do everything themselves; but know what to do if the standard of service they receive does not come up to scratch;

5. be treated better as victims or witnesses to crimes, and have greater confidence that, if they are a victim, the offender will be caught and brought to justice;

6. be clear about the roles which the police and other partners play in tackling anti-social behaviour and crime in communities and how they can be held to account – but also have the opportunity to have a real say in how their local communities are policed with the confidence that their views will be listened to and acted upon;

7. have confidence that the police, local authorities and other agencies are working on their behalf in keeping their communities safe and be aware of and be satisfied with their overall performance in doing so – but also know the part they can play in keeping themselves, their families and their communities safe – and be encouraged to take action and responsibility themselves;

8. be treated professionally, fairly, and with respect and integrity by the police – and know how to complain if this is not the case; and see a police service which is truly representative of the community it serves;

9. be satisfied that taxpayers' money is being spent on the issues of most direct relevance to their safety and well-being; and

10. be confident that the Government is providing support in terms of resources, powers, equipment and ensuring the overall effectiveness of policing – and that it is driving a reduction in bureaucracy.

How we will make this happen

The Government will deliver these commitments through:

1. the spread of dedicated neighbourhood policing teams across the country using the latest real time data and intelligence and backed up by the latest technology and supported by our Neighbourhood Policing Fund. We will deliver 25,000 community support officers and wardens by 2008 in addition to the Government's commitment to maintaining officer numbers;

2. new customer service standards implemented in all police forces by 2006 – which will be built on locally by contracts with communities which will set out the quality of service local people can expect to receive when they contact the police; and the introduction of a new statutory Victims Code of Practice to improve the standard of service that victims of crime receive from the police and other criminal justice agencies;

3. introduction of a single (three digit) non-emergency telephone number and a national strategy to improve call handling and response;

4. all households receiving relevant information about local policing issues;

5. clearer, stronger arrangements for holding the police and other responsible agencies to account for their performance in tackling crime, anti-social behviour and ensuring community safety;

6. a requirement on the police and other agencies to work directly with local people to identify the problems that are most important to them – giving people real opportunities to have a say in local policing priorities;

7. introduction of a new mechanism to trigger a response by the police and other responsible agencies to particular or persistent local problems of crime or anti-social behaviour;

8. improved training across the police service; changing the way police performance is measured to include public satisfaction; and with the new National Policing Improvement Agency supporting and encouraging a new culture of customer responsiveness at all levels within the police service;

9. a particular role within local authorities for 'advocates' to support the public and ensure their voice is heard on community safety issues; and

10. the Government's continuing focus on police performance; more flexible working by the police, greater civilianisation and reducing bureaucracy to deliver the equivalent of 12,000 officers to the frontline by 2008.

What will reform mean to those working in the police?

10 Commitments to the police service

For police officers and police staff, the Government believes that reform should mean the police service in this country:

1. having the support, engagement, respect and confidence of the public;

2. being freed up from bureaucratic burdens with unnecessary paperwork removed whilst maintaining a professional, accountable, thorough approach to apprehending offenders; with more police officers and police staff on the frontline supported by better IT and scientific improvements;

3. knowing that a customer service culture is both supported and valued within the police service – along with the promotion of innovative thinking and continuous professional improvement;

4. being confident that policing is being supported properly by Government – with officers and staff having the resources, powers – and equipment they need to do their jobs effectively;

5. having the flexibility to respond to, and deliver on, the things which most matter to their local communities;

6. being properly recognised and rewarded for the jobs they do;

7. being part of a more unified, integrated workforce – which is not hampered by outdated assumptions about hierarchy and status and where the best people get selected for each role; and with excellent training, learning, support and management being the norm at all levels;

8. working in an environment which respects diversity – and in which racism, sexism, homophobia and other inappropriate behaviour is freely and openly challenged and decisive action taken against offenders – and being part of a service which is truly representative of the communities it serves;

9. working in genuine partnership with others – whose roles and responsibilities in terms of community safety are clear – and who are accountable for their performance in fulfilling their responsibilities; and

10. being confident that there is a structure for, and approach to, policing which enables forces to tackle crime effectively from the very local to the force national and international level with more joined up and effective working between criminal justice agencies.

How we will make this happen

The Government will deliver these commitments through:

1. the spread of dedicated neighbourhood policing and new methods of engagement leading to a deeper, stronger connection with the public;

2. continuing to remove unnecessary bureaucracy and offering practical assistance to forces by way of continuing improvements in scientific and technical support and the further modernisation of police powers;

3. the implementation of improved learning and development programmes for everyone in the service with national standards for Performance and Development Reviews forming the basis of coherent career development and progression; removing the existing requirement for officers to have spent a specific number of years in a particular rank before being eligible for promotion and developing identifiable career pathways for all the extension of work-based assessments for promotion as alternative to exams;

4. new, more family-friendly probationer training arrangements; the accreditation and recognition of prior learning and a national qualification for officers who complete their probations; a Core Leadership Development Programme which will improve the managerial, leadership and operational skills of police officers – focused particularly on police constables – and police staff; improved training for community support officers to better tackle anti-social behaviour and enhanced training leading to a specialist qualification for people wishing to take on Basic Command Unit commander roles;

5. multiple points of entry to the police service above the level of constable for those who can meet the relevant occupational standards;

6. removing barriers for police staff to become police officers in accordance with National Recruitment Standards and enhancing the skills and roles of police staff;

7. maintaining officer numbers and investment; increasing the flexibility of deployment of police officers and staff through better management of shift patterns;

8. the rationalisation of existing national policing bodies and the establishment of a National Policing Improvement Agency to develop good practice and work with forces to provide capacity, assistance and operational policing support – including on the development of officers and staff;

9. recruitment of officers with specific language skills; establishing a national panel of recruitment assessors from ethnic minority communities; more support for serving officers from ethnic minorities; targets for the progression of women in the service; and the introduction of a new Race and Diversity Learning and Development Programme and a duty of police authorities to promote diversity; and

10. greater freedom and autonomy where police forces and Basic Command Units have earned this through effective performance – including an 'inspection break' on a rolling 12 month basis and additional funding freedoms on targets for forces deemed to be graded excellent.

When and how will change happen?

1.40 The Government is clear about its role in setting the national direction and strategic framework for policing in England and Wales. This is a dynamic and fast-moving environment. We have developed our agenda for further change very much in dialogue with the police service and its partners. We do not believe that a Royal Commission on police reform – which some have called for – is desirable, for the simple reason that it would not produce quickly enough the answers and the demonstrable improvements for communities which we desire.[9] The Government is clear that it should set the pace of further improvement. It is the role of Government to ensure equity and the provision of good services to communities across the country. This policy paper is part of that process.

1.41 The Government recognises though that further improvements in policing will not happen overnight. Some of the proposals in this paper will require legislation – which we will progress as soon as Parliamentary time allows. Others will need further discussion, refinement and piloting. And some improvements hinge, in part, on changes in society itself – such as the way our children are brought up, educated and develop. But we think that other changes can, and should, be made now. We are committed to working with police forces, police authorities, their partner agencies, other Government Departments and communities to ensure that people truly see and feel improvements.

1.42 The detail of *how* the Government intends to deliver its vision for a better police service for the 21st century is set out in the remaining chapters of this paper. In taking forward the proposals in this paper, we are mindful of the implications for council tax. The full financial implications of the proposals set out here will become clearer as we develop these policies further. We will need to consider where costs and savings fall in the light of the accepted approach to funding new burdens. The key proposals for change are summarised in Chapter Six and in the accompanying leaflets, available at: www.policereform.gov.uk. But first we begin by examining the progress to date in improving policing and the case for further reform. This is set out in the following Chapter.

---

[9] The last Royal Commission on policing began in 1960 and did not report until 1962.

Chapter Two: More effective policing – progress to date and the case for further reform

Chapter Two: More effective policing – progress to date and the case for further reform

This chapter considers progress to date in improving policing in England and Wales; why further reform is necessary; and the lines along which this should develop in order to ensure that the police service of the rapidly changing 21st century is equipped to meet the needs of those it serves.

Reform does not begin here – progress to date

2.1 Policing in England and Wales is no stranger to reform. The last forty years have seen significant changes in the way policing is structured and carried out in this country.

2.2 The proposals set out in this paper represent the next important step in this Government's sustained programme to improve policing. We published a previous policy paper on police reform in December 2001, with clear proposals to improve police performance, modernise the pay and conditions of officers and take forward the process of modernising the police workforce.[1] We said at the time that the 2001 policy paper did not represent a one-off change for policing in England and Wales. The same is true of this paper. But in putting forward our proposals, we are clear that we are building on firm foundations and real success.

Key successes

The police service, supported by the Government, has already delivered key successes:

- Overall crime has fallen by 30% since 1997, with particularly significant drops in the key volume crimes of burglary and vehicle theft.

- The likelihood of being a victim of crime is at its lowest level for well over 20 years and people's fear of crime is now declining.

- Police numbers are at an all time high, reaching almost 140,000 in August 2004 – 12,570 more than in March 1997. There are also record numbers of police staff – 67,500 – and 4,000 community support officers.

- Government funding for policing has increased by 21% in real terms since March 1997.

- We have overseen the national implementation of the National Intelligence Model as the core way of doing operational business.

---

[1] *Policing a New Century: A Blueprint for Reform* (Cm 5326).

Key successes (continued)

- We have invested approximately £650 million at national level in supporting victims of crime, as well as giving new rights to victims and reforming the Criminal Justice System to provide better support for victims and witnesses from charge, through the trial process and beyond.

- A much stronger performance culture is now embedded within the police service.

- A new Independent Police Complaints Commission began work in April 2004.

- Amongst other ground-breaking developments, we have developed a world-leading National DNA database, which currently holds approximately 2.6 million DNA profiles.

2.3 The Government has also recognised the central importance of effective partnership working. We have established, for example, Local Criminal Justice Boards to bring together agencies like the police, the Crown Prosecution Service, the courts, probation and prison services and Youth Offending Teams. Through their partnership work, nearly 7% more offences were brought to justice in 2003-04 than in 2001-02. We have also enshrined a partnership approach to community safety in the Crime and Disorder Act 1998. There are now 354 increasingly effective Crime and Disorder Reduction Partnerships (CDRPs) in England and 22 Community Safety Partnerships in Wales, bringing key agencies together to contribute to sustained reductions in crime. The 1998 Act also introduced Anti-Social Behaviour Orders (ASBOs) to help protect communities from the kind of thuggish behaviour which can blight people's lives.

2.4 Of the successes listed above, the Government regards two particular issues to be critical parts of the bedrock on which the proposals in this paper for further improvement will be built:

- **police performance** – raising the performance of the police, and reducing the variations in levels of performance between forces, has been at the heart of the Government's agenda. We have seen a true performance culture start to take hold within forces, driven by the complementary work of the Police Standards Unit which we established in June 2001 and by Her Majesty's Inspectorate of Constabulary. Government, police forces, police authorities and, importantly, the public now have access to meaningful, effective local information about forces' performance in comparison with other similar forces. This has ensured systematic and widespread improvement. A sharp focus on raising performance will remain vital to the Government's approach to improving the overall effectiveness of policing, for the benefit of all communities.

- **National Intelligence Model (NIM)** – the Government sees the nation-wide adoption by the police service of the National Intelligence Model – which is about the professional management of intelligence to help direct policing operations – as the single most significant nationally implemented change in policing since 1997. Driven forward by the police service itself, it has been a vital step forward in terms of moving away from a reactive police service and towards one which can anticipate, prevent and fight crime more effectively at every level through the systematic build up of intelligence.

2.5 We explore these two issues further in Chapter Five of this paper.

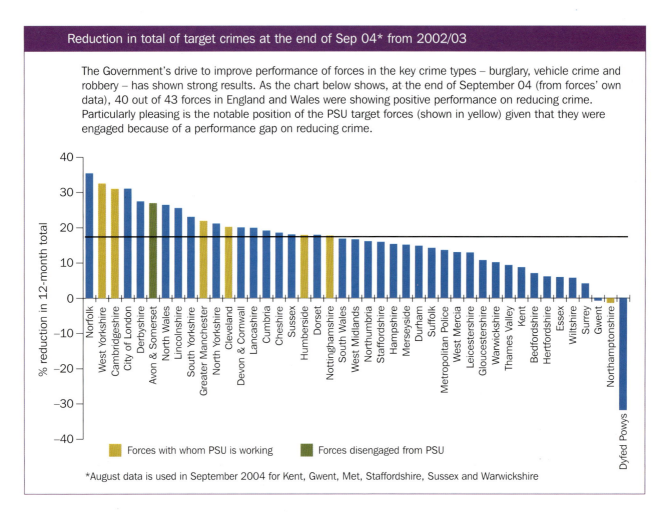

Reduction in total of target crimes at the end of Sep 04* from 2002/03

The Government's drive to improve performance of forces in the key crime types – burglary, vehicle crime and robbery – has shown strong results. As the chart below shows, at the end of September 04 (from forces' own data), 40 out of 43 forces in England and Wales were showing positive performance on reducing crime. Particularly pleasing is the notable position of the PSU target forces (shown in yellow) given that they were engaged because of a performance gap on reducing crime.

% reduction in 12-month total

Forces: Norfolk, West Yorkshire, Cambridgeshire, City of London, Derbyshire, Avon & Somerset, North Wales, Lincolnshire, South Yorkshire, Greater Manchester, North Yorkshire, Cleveland, Devon & Cornwall, Lancashire, Cumbria, Cheshire, Sussex, Humberside, Dorset, Nottinghamshire, South Wales, West Midlands, Northumbria, Staffordshire, Hampshire, Merseyside, Durham, Suffolk, Metropolitan Police, West Mercia, Leicestershire, Gloucestershire, Warwickshire, Thames Valley, Kent, Bedfordshire, Hertfordshire, Essex, Wiltshire, Surrey, Gwent, Northamptonshire, Dyfed Powys

■ Forces with whom PSU is working ■ Forces disengaged from PSU

*August data is used in September 2004 for Kent, Gwent, Met, Staffordshire, Sussex and Warwickshire

Why is further change necessary?

2.6 The early 21st century is a time of rapid change for the world in which we live. From trade to communication to travel, our modern world is defined by being able to do things, buy things and reach places more quickly and easily than ever before. We now live in a genuinely fast-moving information age where, as a society, we are increasingly confident of asserting our rights as individuals, consumers and citizens.

2.7 The demands which this changing world puts on the police service are substantial. The use of modern technology to move money between countries at the push of a button is an essential part of the financial industries which provide so much of this country's prosperity. But the potential they offer to organised criminals is considerable. The increase in cheap and easy travel has provided simpler ways to traffic drugs and people and made it easier for criminals to disappear. And the international terrorist networks, which our police service does so much to combat with the security and intelligence services, thrive on the freedoms offered by the modern world in their attempts to destroy it.

2.8 The scale of this change reflects itself in the way individuals, families and communities feel about their safety and security. Despite the major falls since 1997 in exactly the types of crime most likely to affect people personally – burglary, car theft and robbery – fear of crime, though declining, has not fallen in equal measure. The Government believes this partly reflects particular problems with anti-social behaviour, which it is working hard to address. But it also highlights the fears and insecurities resulting from the rapid changes which our society has gone through over the last ten years.

2.9 These factors are, in themselves, significant drivers for further change. And they form the backdrop to the approach contained in this paper of making policing better and bringing about

further reductions in crime and anti-social behaviour and people's fear of crime and anti-social behaviour. The Government sees some specific challenges here, which we explore below. It is these challenges which this policy paper is seeking to meet in order to achieve the overall objective of beating crime and building communities.

Crime is falling – but it is still too high

2.10 Overall crime has fallen by 30% since 1997 – including a fall of 5% in the last year.[2] The risk of becoming a victim of crime is at its lowest level since the British Crime Survey (BCS) began in 1981 and is one-quarter lower than in 1997, which means 3.3 million fewer people falling victim to crime now than just seven years ago.[3] When compared with other European cities, London comes out on top in a number of categories, including low crime rates.[4] The Government's focus on 'volume crimes' such as burglary, robbery and vehicle crime has led to particularly noticeable results. For example, the action of the police supported by the Crime Reduction Programme, which has funded over 170 projects at a cost of £340 million, has helped to reduce burglary by 42% since 1997. And the Street Crime Initiative, which has involved a wide-range of agencies (including businesses such as mobile telephone companies) working in partnership to deliver a programme of practical measures in response to a sharp rise in robbery, has resulted in a 24% fall in robbery in the 10 police force areas involved in the initiative during its first two years, with robbery continuing to fall.[5] These achievements

---

[2] Based on interviews in the British Crime Survey for the 12 months to March 2004 compared to the 12 months to March 2003.

[3] *Crime in England and Wales 2003-2004.*

[4] Eurostat (European Union's official statistical body) which is produced every 5 years. The analysis confirmed London as the only city in Europe able to compete on the world stage with cities such as New York and Tokyo.

[5] *Crime in England and Wales Quarterly Update 2004* – recorded crime figures show a 15% decline in robbery in England and Wales in April to June 2004 compared with a year earlier.

highlight both the importance and the potential of partnership working in tackling crime. They also demonstrate the clear role for Government in identifying issues of public concern, determining clear objectives and galvanising key partners in order to bring about improvements.

2.11 However, while these successes are real and substantial, crime in England and Wales remains too high, both in absolute terms and in comparison with other European countries and North America.[6] That is why we have committed ourselves through the new Public Service Agreement target from April 2005 to reduce crime by a further 15% from 2002-03 to 2007-08, and by more in high crime areas, with a particular focus on targeting prolific and priority offenders.[7]

Prolific and other Priority Offenders Strategy

Home Office research indicates that the most prolific 5,000 offenders in England and Wales commit some 8-9% of all crime. That is why the Government has developed a strategy focused on preventing young people from becoming prolific offenders, as well as targeting those who are already prolific offenders in order to put an end, once and for all to the havoc they create for the communities in which they live. The strategy, which involves a range of agencies targeting their efforts on this key group of offenders, went live nationally in September 2004.

2.12 The make-up of violent crime and the extent to which it comes to the attention of the police represents a particular challenge in the fight against crime. The number of violent incidents has fallen by 36% since a peak in 1995 and is currently stable. Half of all violent incidents reported to the British Crime Survey did not result in any injury to the victim. Nevertheless, violence committed by strangers has not reduced, whilst violent crimes recorded by the police are rising, with inevitable consequences for people's sense of insecurity. Gun crime represents a particular area of public concern – while the overall level of gun crime in this country is relatively low and the most recent figures indicate some levelling off, there has been a rise in recorded gun crime.

2.13 Demand on the police is also affected by drug use. Drug testing of arrestees in pilot sites in England and Wales suggests that users of heroin, crack and/or cocaine commit six times more offences than non-drug users.[8] Added to this, an increase in the consumption of alcohol, especially amongst women and young people, has placed new demands on the police. Almost half of all violent crime is alcohol related.[9] Alcohol-fuelled crime and disorder is particularly manifested in the night-time drinking culture in town and city centres, resulting in increased levels of demand for policing in these areas. That is why the Government, through a joint ACPO/Police Standards Unit led campaign which has been undertaken in partnership with the Department for Culture, Media and Sport, the

---

[6] The most recent International Crime Victim Survey from 2000 indicates a higher level of crime, especially violent crime, compared to these other countries. The International Crime Victim Survey is a standardised survey, which uses exactly the same questions in all participating countries, carefully translated where necessary.

[7] The Office of the Deputy Prime Minister's fire PSA target, which is to reduce the number of accidental fire-related deaths in the home by 20% and the number of deliberate fires by 2010, contributes to this crime PSA.

[8] Holloway and Bennett (2004) The results of the first two years of the NEW-ADAM programme. Home Office.

[9] Goverrnment Alcohol Harm Reduction Strategy 2004.

Knives

The growing use of knives is another issue of increasing public concern to which the police and other agencies must respond. Figures in relation to homicide show that homicides involving a sharp instrument are in the largest single category of homicides and, although the proportion of total homicides which they represent is lower than 10 years ago, the number has been rising by small amounts since 1996 and rose sharply in 2001-02. Metropolitan Police Service data shows that there were nearly 6,600 knife-related crimes in 2004, which represents an 18% increase compared to 2003. Clearly these statistics call for action. That is why:

- We are seeking to fill the gap in our knowledge about the extent and nature of knife crime as a first step towards an evidence-based strategy. Work at community level is likely to form a substantial part of the strategy, as it has with our work on tackling gun crime.

- The Metropolitan Police Service intends to undertake an initiative to deter young people from carrying knives on the streets of London. This was initially piloted in three Boroughs and is due to be rolled out shortly across the remaining 29 London Boroughs.

- Work is on going with the Department for Education and Skills, the Home Office, ACPO and schools on how and when the police might be used to augment preventative and culture-changing measures in schools.

- We are looking at where existing legislation might be tightened.

The growing number of incidents of crimes involving knives must be checked. The Government is fully committed to driving down this trend to make our communities, streets and schools safer.

Local Authorities Co-ordinators of Regulatory services, the alcohol industry and trading standards officers, has cracked down hard on issues such as binge and underage drinking, with initially very encouraging results. A new campaign is planned for the Christmas/New Year period. The Licensing Act 2003 will encourage well-run premises to offer alcohol at more flexible opening hours, while bearing down heavily on those premises considered to be too lenient in dealing with drunkenness, binge-drinking and disorderly behaviour.

2.14 Tied to the commitment to reduce crime is a desire on the part of the Government to reduce people's fear of crime. Although both crime and the fear of crime have fallen, people's perception that crime is <u>actually</u> falling – and in turn their sense of security – remains too low.[10] Violent crime bears some responsibility for this perception. But for many people it is the kind of anti-social behaviour and disorder they see taking place unchecked in their neighbourhoods which dominates their perceptions.

---

[10] Findings from the BCS 2003-04 show that fear of crime has fallen compared with the previous year, with falls in the proportion of people with high levels of worry about burglary, car crime and vehicle crime. However, despite this reduction, 48% of the public still thought that crime in their area had increased over the previous year.

2.15 Respect for each other and the areas in which we live is at the heart of strong communities. Anti-social behaviour undermines our communities, creating an environment of fear and neglect where more serious crime can take hold. It is for these reasons that the Government has placed a very high priority on tackling anti-social behaviour. Largely as a result of this emphasis – and of initiatives such as the TOGETHER campaign[11] and Anti-Social Behaviour Prosecutors which have derived from it – public concern about the problem of anti-social behaviour is now falling.[12] But, as with other issues around tackling crime and disorder, more needs to be done. That is why, in addition to the ten "Trailblazer" areas already established, dedicated anti-social behaviour resources and support are to be introduced in a further 50 action areas.[13] If we are to reduce insecurity and the fear of crime, the police and their local partners must keep up the momentum in tackling anti-social behaviour – to shift the balance of power from the minority who spread fear and distress to the majority who want to win back their neighbourhoods for themselves and their children.

The British Crime Survey

The British Crime Survey provides the most complete, reliable and robust assessment of crime, covering all crime including both reported and unreported crime.[14] The survey is conducted through 50,000 interviews each year, making it one of the largest surveys in the UK, and its high quality design provides results of the highest level of statistical accuracy available.[15] The BCS asks interviewees how often they have been victims of crime and elicits their perceptions and fears. The same questions are asked each year, allowing a 'like for like' comparison of patterns of crime over time.

2.16 The British Crime Survey (BCS) is central to being able to measure crime and the fear of crime accurately. The BCS measures crime as people experience it, providing a very reliable indicator of crime levels and trends, as well as how to tackle these effectively in a way which will then impact positively on perception.

---

[11] "Together: Tackling Anti-Social Behaviour" – details available at www.homeoffice.gov.uk/crime/antisocialbehaviour

[12] The BCS for 2003-04 showed that 16% of people in England and Wales perceived a high level of disorder in their local areas, a reduction from the corresponding figure of 22% in 2002-03.

[13] Confident Communities in a Secure Britain – page 15.

[14] In 2003/2004, the BCS estimated that only 42% of incidents were reported to the police and this figure varied considerably across crime types.

[15] Both the criminological and policing communities respect the BCS as an authoritative and reliable measure of crime trends. Many police forces use the survey as a tool for designing their own surveys. The BCS has also been widely used by academics.

The British Crime Survey (continued)

In contrast, **recorded crime** – as reported to the police – is affected by how willing the public is to report crime. It is also influenced by changes in rules and practices for recording crime by the police, providing therefore a less robust comparative measure. As a result of continuing differences between forces in recording, the Association of Chief Police Officers developed a new National Crime Recording Standard (NCRS), to bring greater consistency between areas, which was adopted across all police forces from April 2002. NCRS, in combination with increasing public confidence in reporting crime, has led to the recording of more offences in some areas. As a result, much crime is now being recorded which was not previously registered and monitored, allowing the police to respond effectively to areas of greatest concern. These developments mean that while overall crime levels have fallen substantially, the proportion of those recorded by the police has risen.[16]

2.17 Policing in England and Wales must accordingly be responsive both to levels of crime and to the factors which contribute to them. The police reform programme must enable rather than inhibit such responsive policing in order to maximise the ability of the police to spot new crime and social trends and respond quickly and effectively to them. Community intelligence, supported by the National Intelligence Model and up to date modern policing methods such as real time data, is fundamental and, to be fully responsive, the police service must work closely with the communities it serves. That is why our plans for further reform of the police service, as set out in the remainder of this paper, focus on how the police can develop and encourage the type of neighbourhood policing which can help continue to bring down crime, while tackling people's fears and insecurities effectively.

Increasing the responsiveness and customer service of the police

Neighbourhood Policing

2.18 Focused local policing, with a community which is genuinely engaged, is essential to fighting crime and building a stronger society. A community that feels it is part of the solution can work successfully with its local policing team to play a real part in reducing crime and anti-social behaviour. That is why the Government is committed to providing effective, accessible neighbourhood policing to deliver increased confidence and security. The pledge for community support officers to be available in every town and city by 2008 to complement the work of police officers is a part of this. But

---

[16] It is estimated that the crimes counted in 2002/2003 were 10% higher than they would have been under pre-NCRS recording, particularly in relation to violent crimes against the person, reflecting a change in recording practice as opposed to a real increase in crime.

effective neighbourhood policing is about more than just more 'bobbies on the beat'. It is about dedicated resources for neighbourhoods, which are used to respond to neighbourhood level priorities. Central to this is engagement with communities, with a focus on public involvement not only in identifying problems but in prioritising action and shaping and participating in solutions. Neighbourhood policing is what communities want, as was made clear in response to 'Policing: Building Safer Communities Together',[17] and we expect to see forces and authorities continue to adopt the neighbourhood policing approach considered in detail in Chapter Three.

Customer service

2.19 A necessary first step towards this approach – as well as being of fundamental importance in its own right – is creating a more customer-focused police service, in which members of the public feel satisfaction and confidence. If people feel confidence in the police they are more likely to be prepared to help them, for example by acting as a witness. They are also more likely to actively engage in the fight against crime.

2.20 Compared with some other professions, the police continue to be held in high regard – the highest of all of the Criminal Justice System agencies. However, despite the fact that police numbers are now at historically high levels, public satisfaction with policing – while still high overall – is declining. In 2002-03, 75% of people felt that the police in their area did a good job, compared with 82% and 92% in 1992 and 1982 respectively.[19] And, unlike services such as hospitals and schools, when people have contact with the police, their confidence in the service declines. This is a worrying situation given the key role that the police play within communities.

2.21 It is particularly worrying in its application to victims and witnesses.[19] Evidence shows, not surprisingly, that how the police respond to victims and witnesses determines whether or not they continue to engage with the criminal justice process. Getting this right is therefore vital not only to increasing the satisfaction of victims and witnesses but also in bringing more offences to justice. There has been a strong commitment both nationally and locally to improving the Criminal Justice System for victims and witnesses and much progress has been made. But clearly there is much more still to be done to ensure that the police provide the high quality service which victims and witnesses rightly expect.

2.22 The Government is committed, therefore, to improving public satisfaction and confidence in the police, including that of victims and witnesses, wherever and whenever contact takes place. In order to be effective, the police need to be able to perform their duties with the active co-operation, not just consent, of local communities. This means exercising these duties fairly and effectively. Use of the police powers to stop and search in a way in which communities have trust and confidence is a critical case in point.

---

[17] *Policing: Building Safer Communities Together – Summary of Consultation Responses* – available at www.policereform.gov.uk

[18] British Crime Survey (BCS)

[19] Victim satisfaction with the police dropped by 10% between 1994 and 2002 and black and minority ethnic victim satisfaction with the police is much lower than amongst white respondents.

Stop and Search

The Government supports the police powers of stop and search and believes them to be an important tool in the prevention and detection of crime when used in a targeted and intelligence-led way. The Government is clear that these powers must also be applied in the least bureaucratic way possible. However, coupled with this is the need to bring greater accountability, openness and transparency to this area of policing and to maintain the trust and confidence of communities in the powers of stop and search. That is why the Home Secretary has set an end date of 1st April 2005 by which all forces must be recording stops – a requirement which arises from Recommendation 61 of the Stephen Lawrence Inquiry Report.

The Government has set up a Stop and Search Action Team to ensure both that the use of stop and search powers is fair and as effective as possible in the prevention and detection of crime, and that the powers are being used proportionately. The team has been tasked with bringing about practical change on the ground by reducing the unequal use of stop and search in relation to different groups of the population and increasing community confidence in this police power. As part of its work programme, the Stop and Search Action Team has commissioned research into the fairness of police practices, targeting and different groups' use of public space. This research will be used to inform policy proposals on measuring disproportionality. The Stop and Search Manual, for use by the police service and police authorities, will be published in Spring 2005.

2.23 Improving public satisfaction and confidence also means doing more to improve the customer-service provided by the police – how people are treated when they visit police stations, for example, or when they telephone the police. In recent baseline assessments of forces by Her Majesty's Inspectorate of Constabulary,[20] call handling was ranked second to bottom of the components of policing being inspected and no forces were ranked as excellent. These findings in part reflect the fact that the police provide the only 24 hours a day response number. They are nonetheless unsatisfactory. Serious improvement is needed and this, including the development of national minimum standards of quality of service and the establishment of a single three-digit non-emergency number for accessing local services, is considered in greater detail in Chapter Three of this paper.

Community engagement

2.24 Creating a more responsive and customer-focused police service is also integral to the Government's vision of strong, active and empowered communities which, amongst other things, can take a shared responsibility for preventing and reducing crime. Economic and social regeneration go hand in hand with both providing basic security and building confidence within the community to be part of the solution. This includes engaging with people to ensure the basic security of their homes and cars and raising people's confidence and therefore preparedness to help the police. But it is also about much more. The police must work with local communities to tackle local problems and work in partnership to deliver real change, instilling a sense of responsibility and moving away from a passive dependency culture.

---

[20] The baseline assessment process is a new methodology reflecting the changing environment in which police forces and authorities are operating. It is designed to set out comprehensively the strengths of each force and the areas where it should improve. The assessments are available at www.homeoffice.gov.uk/hmic/ba.htm#summaries

2.25 That is why the Government is committed to giving local people a greater say in determining local community safety priorities and building their capacity and opportunities to participate in reducing crime. In part, this will involve developing and encouraging engagement that already exists. Successful burglary reduction schemes, for example, have tended to include residents as stakeholders and effective community engagement. Special constables are a very real example of active citizens, offering their time and skills to improve local safety. Neighbourhood Watch, which the Government is committed to strengthening and revitalising, plays a key role in crime prevention. And there are already new ways of working with communities – such as Street Leaders in Southwark and community 'guardians' in Leicestershire – identifiable across the country. However, giving local people a greater say will also involve introducing new methods of engagement, such as giving people the ability to "trigger" action in response to local problems, which are considered further in Chapter Three of this paper.

Southwark Street Leaders

The Southwark Street Leaders scheme is one of a number of initiatives which seek to make the borough's neighbourhoods cleaner and safer. Set up in 2003, the scheme operates as a partnership between more than 100 local residents and a team of Southwark Council support staff. Street Leaders volunteer to keep an eye on the streets they pass through whilst going about their day to day lives. They make a commitment to report any 'environmental crimes' and eye-sores such as dog mess, graffiti and fly-tipping to the council, which then ensures that the problem gets dealt with quickly.

Building a modernised police workforce

2.26 The key measure of reform and indicator of success for a public service must always be whether or not the public itself sees and feels a difference. However, whether the police service feels that improvements have been made is also important. Building a modernised police workforce is central to this. It is also integral to the delivery of the responsive, customer-focused policing described above.

2.27 Much progress has already been made. The total police workforce now stands at nearly 225,000, compared with 192,000 in March 2000, and these record resources are increasingly being deployed to boost the proportion of time which skilled, trained police officers can spend on frontline policing. The Government and the police service have, for example, improved the status, training and legal framework for police staff in order to enhance their ability and ease the burden on police officers. An increasing number of civilian staff are undertaking station-based tasks such as case preparation, which would previously have been allocated to officers. We have introduced more flexible pay and conditions. And we have gone some way to reducing red tape, with over 7,700 forms now obsolete across all 43 forces.

These changes will help the Government to meet its commitment to free up the equivalent of at least 12,000 officers to the frontline by 2007-08.[21]

2.28 However, although progress has been made, the Government realises that more radical change is needed if the police service is to be enabled to build a truly modernised police workforce. The service and the Government must do more, for example, to eradicate unnecessary bureaucracy within the service. Further training and development for the whole police workforce is vital if we are to achieve the culture change necessary to introduce a truly modern and responsive police service. And we remain particularly interested in the greater empowerment and development of police leaders at Basic Command Unit level.

2.29 One of the biggest challenges which we face, as the "Secret Policeman" documentary showed only too clearly, is rooting out racism and creating a genuinely open and diverse police service. There is no place for racism or any other form of discrimination in a modern and responsive service. Eradicating this involves not only identifying and removing discrimination within the police service but also actively promoting diversity within the service so that it can mirror, and draw strength from, the diversity of the communities which it polices. This, along with our other proposals to build a more modern police workforce, is considered further in Chapter Four of this paper.

Ensuring effective policing from local to national level

2.30 At the heart of our reform programme is the desire to create a more responsive and customer-focused police service. However, if we are to fully succeed in achieving this we must also ensure that we have the right national infrastructure, organisation, resources, policing methods and legal framework for the police to fight crime at all levels, including the national and international threats posed by organised crime and terrorism. This should be seen in the context of an increasingly complex and insecure world, whose challenges must be met if we are to create and maintain a safe and secure society. The growth of organised crime and the changing terrorist threat have demanded a significant shift in the way we operate.

Terrorism

2.31 Clearly terrorism is not a new concept. It is, however, qualitatively and quantitatively different in nature to the past, as ACPO highlighted in their National Strategic Assessment published in May 2004.[22] The nature of the threat has changed since the September 11 attacks: it is now not only from established groups with clearly defined targets, but also from loose-knit networks of individuals with a far broader agenda. We now face international terrorists with a high degree of loyalty to their cause, intent on causing mass casualties and willing to mount suicide attacks, which means policing methods can no longer count on the terrorist wanting to escape unharmed. The Al Qaeda terrorism network, for example, may strike anywhere, at anytime and using any means. Terrorism remains, therefore, one of the most challenging crimes facing police forces nationally. As we made clear in the Home Office Strategic Plan, doing everything possible to prevent a major act of terrorism on UK soil is the single biggest responsibility for the Home Office, the Security Service and the police.

---

[21] Confident Communities in a Secure Britain – page 65.

[22] Available at www.acpo.police.uk

2.32 That is why the Government has put a large amount of resources and effort into the fight against terrorism. An additional £330 million was provided for counter-terrorism and policing in the 2002 budget. There will be an extra 1,000 staff in the Security Service by 2008. And there has been a significant expansion of Special Branches, with an additional £90 million of funding allocated for 2005. We have also undertaken a major overhaul of protective security and resilience arrangements; set up the Asset Recovery Agency, with tough powers to seize assets from organised criminals; and toughened our laws to give the police the powers they need, including extending the time available to question terrorist suspects from 7 to 14 days, which has already proven its worth.

2.33 So, much has already been done – but we cannot relax our efforts if we are to defeat the ongoing terrorist threat. The consultation paper published in February 2004, in which we set out some ideas on how to modernise and broaden further our anti-terrorism laws, should be seen in this context.[23] The same is so of the continued regionalisation and co-ordination of Special Branches to match the expansion of the Security Service. On top of this, we will be making it more difficult for terrorists to use fraudulent identities through our plan to introduce biometric identity cards by 2008. Together with our investment in high-tech border controls, this will complement the tough laws which have already deterred terrorists from using the UK as a base.

Organised crime

2.34 Organised crime has also become increasingly developed and sophisticated, again fuelled by the changing world in which we live. The use of new technologies such as the internet creates new criminal opportunities like viruses, hacking and denial of computer service, as well as making scams, fraud and trade in illegal goods cheaper and more effective to carry out on a national and international basis. These new technologies also enable crimes such as paedophilia and people trafficking to be carried to new levels of speed and sophistication. Increased travel and migration and more mobile communities have also contributed to this growing sophistication. Organised criminals have, for example, taken advantage of easier travel to bring in more Class A drugs to feed a core group of drug users whose chaotic lives cause crime and anti-social behaviour. As ACPO highlighted in their National Strategic Assessment published in May 2004, the ability of organised criminals to adapt and respond to opportunities and threats make them hard to tackle; the law enforcement response needs to keep pace.

2.35 In response, we have already announced our intention to create the Serious Organised Crime Agency (SOCA) by 2006. This will be a groundbreaking new national organisation bringing together some 5,000 law enforcement agents and specialists, who have up to now worked in a number of separate organisations, in order to stay one step ahead of organised criminals. The challenge in terms of policing will be to ensure that the structures and mechanisms we have in place at police force level will dovetail seamlessly with SOCA, while maintaining crucial connections and collaboration both upwards and between forces.

---

[23] Available at www.homeoffice.gov.uk/terrorism/reports/other/html

Structures and standards

2.36 The Government is very clear that police forces need to be given sufficient flexibility to deliver on local priorities. The new Public Service Agreement target from April 2005 to reduce crime by a further 15%, and by more in high crime areas, from 2002-03 to 2007-08 should be seen in this context. This broader target will give police forces and authorities, together with their communities and partners, greater flexibility to target the crimes that are of the most pressing local concern and which collectively can achieve the shared goal to reduce crime. At the same time, this flexibility has to be set within a context in which the Government remains responsible for setting national standards, priorities and systems to ensure the overall effectiveness of policing in this country. The need for a framework and structure to achieve this is substantiated by the Bichard Report into the Soham murders, which clearly indicated that there is more to do in managing intelligence between forces, and is considered further in Chapter Five of this paper.[24]

2.37 Chapter Five also considers the need for the police service to be answerable to the communities it serves and the importance of this in relation to responsiveness. Home Office research undertaken with the Association of Police Authorities indicates a general consensus that the public does not have a sufficient say in decisions about policing and that people want better communication, information and involvement.[25] The vast majority of people involved in the research had not heard of police authorities. The few that had heard of them generally did not know what they were or what their role was. Responses to *Policing: Building Safer Communities Together* conveyed a similar message, revealing a strong desire from all quarters to ensure that the police were more visible and accessible, to give local people a greater say in determining local community safety priorities and to strengthen accountability in policing. Current arrangements need to be bolstered and simplified to ensure that the public is clear about who is responsible for what, how well they are performing and how they can be held to account. The proposals outlined in both Chapters Three and Five seek to achieve these objectives.

So we need to go further

2.38 Across the public sector we are looking at fundamental reform of how services are delivered to the citizen in a way which combines choice, excellence and equity. We are not looking for "one size fits all" solutions. We will continue to invest in capacity and keep a focus on driving up standards and performance.

2.39 Our aim is to put an entirely different dynamic in place to drive public services: driven by the user – in the case of policing and community safety, by the law-abiding citizen. The remainder of this policy paper sets out our specific proposals to put the law-abiding citizen at the heart of our reform programme. By getting this right we can all play our part in ensuring that the police service of the 21st century is equipped to meet the needs of those it serves.

---

[24] The Government is coordinating a programme of implementation in response to the Bichard Report. Work on this is being taken forward as a matter of urgency with the aim of being able to demonstrate substantial progress by early 2005.

[25] The Role of Public Authorities in Public Engagement, published 4 November 2003 – available at www.homeoffice.gov.uk/rds

Chapter Three: A new relationship between the police and the public – building trust and confidence

Chapter Three: A new relationship between the police and the public – building trust and confidence

What we want to achieve:

- **accessible and responsive neighbourhood policing that is capable of dealing with 21st century challenges of crime and anti-social behaviour across all forces;**

- **every community to benefit from this style of policing and to know who is responsible for their area with dedicated policing teams in place and 25,000 community support officers and wardens by 2008;**

- **a new culture of customer responsiveness within the police service, with guaranteed standards of customer service whenever anyone has contact with the police; and**

- **real opportunities for local communities to have a say in local policing priorities.**

Key proposals:

- programme to roll-out neighbourhood policing across all forces and provide training and skills for police officers and staff, together with a new Neighbourhood Policing Fund;

- continuing drive on reducing bureaucracy to help free up the equivalent of 12,000 officers to the frontline by 2008;

- all forces to implement customer service standards by 2006;

- National Policing Improvement Agency to drive customer service culture in all forces;

- changes in the way police performance is measured to reflect the priorities of the public and their views about police services;

- single non-emergency telephone number and strategy to improve call-handling;

- a requirement on the police and other agencies to work directly with local people to identify and tackle the problems that are most important to them; and

- the right for local communities to trigger action by the relevant agencies to deal with acute or persistent problems of crime and anti-social behaviour.

A new relationship between the police and the public

3.1 The Government's aim is to put people at the centre of public services. With increasing investment, the public rightly has increasing expectations of the quality of the services it receives. Providers of services across the public and private sectors are facing mounting external pressures from a more demanding consumer culture and an environment where communities are becoming increasingly diverse, complex and mobile. Policing is no exception.

3.2 Added to these pressures for change is the place occupied by the police service in our shared idea of community. The local police serve as a focus for communities' sense of safety and security. As well as those who have direct contact with the police, everyone benefits from the services provided by the police on a daily basis. As such the police service has a unique value and importance to the public.

3.3 But the relationship between the public and the police is not only critical to people's feelings of safety, fear of crime or confidence. It is also essential to the continued effectiveness of the police in tackling crime and disorder and bringing offenders to justice. Bringing about safer and more secure communities is dependent on the co-operation and support of members of the public, for example, by people providing information leading to the arrest of criminals involved in dealing drugs and gun crime and acting as witnesses when cases come to court. Local communities are often best placed to find the most appropriate and long-term solutions to problems of crime and anti-social behaviour.

3.4 Forging a new relationship between the police and the public – in which there is active collaboration between the police, their partners and citizens in the delivery of policing services – is the underlying principle on which our proposals are based. We recognise that effective policing will only be sustained over the long term when it is citizen-focused – responsive to people's needs and performed as a shared undertaking *with* the active involvement of the public. But in order to engage and be involved, people must have a basic confidence that they are guaranteed high standards of service; that policing in their area reflects and responds to their needs; and that they have genuine opportunities to become involved on their own terms. The Government recognises that there is already much good work underway in a number of forces that is proving successful. We want to build on this and bring all forces up to the same high standard.

3.5 Tackling crime and reassuring the public go hand in hand – to pursue one at the expense of the other may work in the short term but over the long term is unsustainable. We want a situation where a two-way exchange of information between the police and the public leads to improvements in crime reduction and ever increasing levels of trust and confidence. There are real wins here for the police, the public and society in general.

Neighbourhood policing for today's world

3.6 Revitalising the policing of neighbourhoods for today's world is central to the Government's approach to improving policing in this country. Despite year on year reductions in crime, the public's fear of crime remains too high. Many people are, understandably, not convinced that

Guardians in Leicestershire

The approach to policing in Leicestershire is based upon the philosophy of 'right people, right numbers, right place'. The 'right people' starts with a clear understanding of the fundamental policing role as community 'guardians', where the emphasis is upon relationship building, listening and problem solving.

Every police officer is given their own unique part of Leicestershire to oversee as 'guardian', the size and nature of which depends upon local issues but could be an estate, shopping area or village. Although routine demand means they cannot be present all the time, the 'micro-beat' is a constant default which they must return to and oversee. Promotion, movement into specialist departments and bonuses are increasingly dependent on an officer's impact on improving the quality of life in their area.

crime is going down if they do not see and experience effective and responsive policing themselves – in their neighbourhoods and communities; and when they have contact with the police. A positive experience of policing is also vital to building people's trust and confidence in the police service itself.

3.7   But unlike previous community policing initiatives, the new style of neighbourhood policing being advanced by the Government in partnership with the police service will not just be about delivering public reassurance, as important as that is. Excellent police forces today can and should be about reassuring the public and preventing and detecting crime. And importantly for the Government, its approach to neighbourhood policing involves harnessing the energies of local communities and partners to exchange information and work together to continue to reduce crime and anti-social behaviour and improve the number of crimes detected and offences brought to justice. Establishing effective and responsive neighbourhood policing is essential to making this happen.

How will this approach to neighbourhood policing operate in practice?

3.8   The Government recognises that a number of police forces in England and Wales are already putting in place what is needed for a successful neighbourhood policing approach. We want to build on this good practice.

3.9   The critical starting point for the Government is forces having dedicated teams of police officers and community support officers, working in concert with wardens and other members of what is sometimes referred to as the 'extended police family' to provide a visible and accessible presence in communities. Ongoing workforce modernisation pilot schemes are providing valuable evidence of the impact so-called 'mixed economy' teams can have in neighbourhoods and beyond. We want such teams to develop a genuine sense of being responsible for and 'owning' their local areas. This means the police involving communities in negotiating priorities for action and, together with partners and the communities themselves, finding lasting solutions to local problems. We talk about this kind of engagement further in paragraphs 3.45 onwards below. But more than this, we are clear that neighbourhood policing for today's world must be intelligence-led, which involves the systematic adoption and application of the National Intelligence Model. So along with greater accessibility and responsiveness to people's concerns and needs, the roll-out of neighbourhood policing will mean a more proactive, problem-orientated approach being taken to local issues.

3.10 The Government has been engaged in a programme of pilot initiatives and research to understand the essential elements of a successful neighbourhood policing approach. We have also been able to draw on the experience of forces both in this country and abroad. Neighbourhood policing will not mean a one-size fits all approach, but we believe that effective models will share the following features:

- dedicated resources for neighbourhoods which include the extended police family, but where numbers, staffing mix, skills and powers available are appropriate to the particular needs of the neighbourhood;

- an emphasis on local problem solving with mechanisms in place to identify and respond to neighbourhood level priorities and to draw in additional resources from other levels and partners where necessary;

- engagement with communities, using a range of methods appropriate to the communities concerned;

- a focus on public involvement not only in identifying problems but in prioritising action and shaping and participating in solutions, along with police and partners; and

- mechanisms in place to target resources at local priorities and to hold police and partners to account for tackling neighbourhood problems.

Neighbourhood Policing in Merseyside

In April 2001, Merseyside Police introduced a new style of policing in order to re-engage with the public.

Neighbourhood policing redeploys response officers into dedicated teams in each of forty-three neighbourhoods led by an inspector who is accountable for the policing needs of that community – a mini chief constable of the community. The inspector has a team typically consisting of three sergeants and sixteen constables as well as community support officer support.

The aim was to give residents in Merseyside a familiar and reassuring local police service, empowering communities to determine policing priorities. In order to achieve this, the force needed to completely change its structure and systems, and required a performance focus on public satisfaction and confidence.

In the last three years, crime has not only been reduced, but surveys have shown increases in public satisfaction. Robbery has reduced by 25% and vehicle theft has reduced by 24%. Street interview surveys have shown levels of confidence and satisfaction in the police have risen by 10%.

3.11 Effective neighbourhood policing is therefore about more than satisfying a public desire for more 'bobbies on the beat' and cannot be seen as an activity that stands in isolation from the rest of policing. To be successful, neighbourhood policing needs to apply the same intelligence-led approach that has been so successful at tackling volume crime and serious organised crime. People who are living within communities blighted by violent or drug-related crime know that it is not just 'quality of life issues' that concern local communities. There is not a quick fix. Their priorities often link directly to policing issues which cross force boundaries such as drug importation and trafficking. Many of the problems facing communities have existed for decades and will take time to resolve. But putting in place dedicated neighbourhood teams can build up relationships of trust with local communities over time. These teams are ideally placed to monitor issues and tensions within the community. We see an essential part of their role to be gathering community intelligence, which must be fed into the National Intelligence Model process.

3.12 To be successful – and to avoid replicating the problems with previous approaches to community policing – the Government is clear that its approach to neighbourhood policing must not be seen as some kind of bolt-on or distinct activity by police forces. Effective neighbourhood level policing requires proper integration with other policing functions such as first contact, response, investigation and major crime work. It will therefore need the wholesale commitment of forces to put in place an infrastructure to support it.

Government support for neighbourhood policing

3.13 The Government's ongoing programme of reform is already providing the building blocks for the kind of neighbourhood policing approach set out in this paper. We have, for example, introduced the role of community support officer and made other changes in terms of civilianising police posts and reducing bureaucracy to free up frontline officers' time. The police pay reforms agreed in 2002 provide a way for forces to reward staff in particular posts – like community or neighbourhood officers – in order to attract and, crucially, retain people in those important roles – where continuity is vital. We agree with the sentiment expressed by Lord Scarman in his 1981 Report on the unrest in Brixton that year about enhancing the status of what was then referred to as the beat officer – that they should be seen:

> "…not as occupying the bottom of the police pecking-order… but at its apex, in the forefront of the police team."[1]

---

[1] The Brixton Disorders 10-12 April 1981 – Report of an Inquiry by the Rt.Hon. The Lord Scarman OBE (Cmnd. 8427) – p.90.

3.14 But Lord Scarman saw the beat officer as a generalist position. We believe that in today's environment, the role of a neighbourhood officer should be seen as a highly skilled, specialist one – which needs and deserves proper training and support. As we set out in this paper, whilst the Government sees neighbourhood policing being carried out most effectively by 'mixed' teams, we are clear that it is the police constable who will continue to play the pivotal, problem-solving role within them.

3.15 As we note above, some police forces have already committed themselves to neighbourhood policing and they, and their communities, are starting to feel the impact. But elsewhere, effective and responsive neighbourhood policing is not business as usual. We want communities across the country to benefit from this style of policing and believe that, in addition to investment, the spread of neighbourhood policing requires the development of a supportive infrastructure and an understanding of new tactics. Effective management of a wide range of resources to meet local needs, for example, is key to ensuring the successful and sustainable implementation of the kind of dedicated neighbourhood policing approach set out in this paper.

3.16 In terms of support, the Government will therefore:

- **set out joint guidance on neighbourhood policing for forces with the Association of Chief Police Officers and the National Centre for Policing Excellence early in 2005;**

- **put in place a programme to help forces implement neighbourhood policing and make sure that the highly skilled role of neighbourhood officers is recognised,**

valued and trained in the same way as other specialists within the police service;

- **support the roll-out of neighbourhood policing with substantial investment through the new Neighbourhood Policing Fund. We will deliver 25,000 CSOs and wardens by 2008; and**

- **run a national community policing TOGETHER Academy Programme in March 2005 to ensure police officers and their CSO colleagues have the tools, the know-how and the backing to tackle anti-social behaviour in the communities they serve.**

Investing in neighbourhood policing

3.17 The Government has already injected £50m of new money this year to provide what is, in effect, the first round of the Neighbourhood Policing Fund. This will mean an additional 2,000 CSOs will be recruited by the end of March 2005. We will deliver 25,000 CSOs and wardens by 2008. Forces will receive continuation funding and will be required to maintain police officer numbers to be eligible for Neighbourhood Policing Fund money. The Fund will pay for existing CSOs and for measures being funded already to increase the capacity of the special constabulary. Beyond this, the Neighbourhood Policing Fund is intended to be a flexible investment fund to support the implementation of neighbourhood policing. Unlike the Crime Fighting Fund, the additional money in the Neighbourhood Policing Fund will not simply be used on a "money for people" basis. Police authorities and forces will be invited to set out their plans for the implementation of neighbourhood policing, including a commitment to the number of CSOs they will recruit. But how they use money from the Neighbourhood Policing Fund to achieve this will be up to them.

Neighbourhood Policing Fund

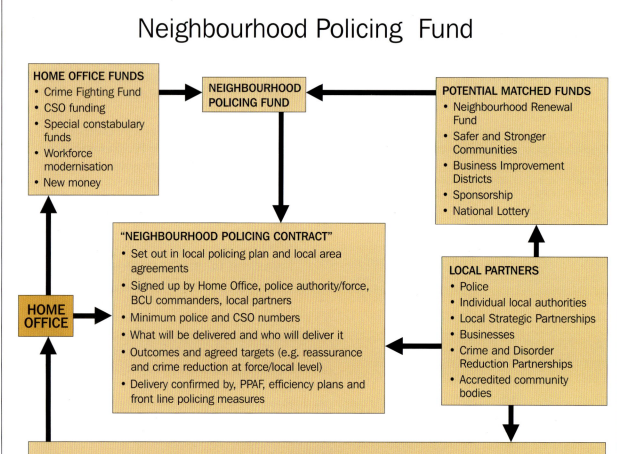

HOME OFFICE FUNDS
- Crime Fighting Fund
- CSO funding
- Special constabulary funds
- Workforce modernisation
- New money

NEIGHBOURHOOD POLICING FUND

POTENTIAL MATCHED FUNDS
- Neighbourhood Renewal Fund
- Safer and Stronger Communities
- Business Improvement Districts
- Sponsorship
- National Lottery

"NEIGHBOURHOOD POLICING CONTRACT"
- Set out in local policing plan and local area agreements
- Signed up by Home Office, police authority/force, BCU commanders, local partners
- Minimum police and CSO numbers
- What will be delivered and who will deliver it
- Outcomes and agreed targets (e.g. reassurance and crime reduction at force/local level)
- Delivery confirmed by, PPAF, efficiency plans and front line policing measures

HOME OFFICE

LOCAL PARTNERS
- Police
- Individual local authorities
- Local Strategic Partnerships
- Businesses
- Crime and Disorder Reduction Partnerships
- Accredited community bodies

PROPOSAL
- Sets out how reassurance contract will be delivered through workforce modernisation, leading to increased front line capacity used to support creation of neighbourhood policing teams (police officers, specials, CSOs, empowered police staff) supported by volunteers, Neighbourhood Watch, community guardians.
- Maintaining police officer and CSO numbers a pre-requisite
- Police authority/force manage preparations of bid and submit it to Home Office on behalf of partners
- Bid at force level but constructed from proposals generated at BCU level
- Bid needs local community support. Evidence of support from LSP, local authority, CDRP, as appropriate. Partners must sign up to bid along with relevant BCU commanders, force and authority
- Matched funding required from community partners or explanation of why there is no matched funding

3.18 The Government will set out the full details of requirements for applications to the Neighbourhood Policing Fund in 2006/07 and 2007/08 in mid 2005.

Reducing bureaucracy

3.19 As part of our drive on neighbourhood policing and supporting the development of a more responsive police service, the Government remains committed to reducing the administrative burdens and eliminating unecessary paperwork and inefficient working practices that keep officers away from the communities they serve. We want to empower officers and equip them to spend time in their core roles – tackling crime and providing reassurance to the public. We are already making progress:

- over 7,700 forms have been made obsolete across all 43 forces;

- all 43 forces now undertake video identity parades to speed up the identification of suspects. It is estimated that it takes 66% less time for a uniformed officer to carry out a video identity parade than a live one. They greatly reduce bureaucracy, are welcomed by forces and, over five years, will represent an overall saving of £143m to the police service;

- over 72,000 police officers and staff are now using the new generation of Airwave radios operationally in 40 forces, and 20 forces are using mobile information. This allows officers to cut down on the amount of time spent returning to the station and is making a significant difference to everyday policing;

- the national roll out of the penalty notice for disorder scheme was completed in April 2004. Over 30,000 such notices had been issued by

the end of September 2004, each one representing a file for court which did not have to be prepared. It is estimated that around 90 minutes is saved per ticket. The scheme is being extended to build on its success. A further 10 offences, including criminal damage and theft, have been added, with CSOs being able to issue penalty notices for disorder for all the new offences, except theft. The scheme is also being extended to tackle disorderly and nuisance offending by juveniles. From 20 January 2005, 16 and 17 year olds will be able to be issued with penalty notices for disorder. We have pased legislation to enable the scheme to be extended to juveniles aged 10 to 15 years of age and pilots are expected to start later in 2004;

- 198 Livescan Units, which enable electronic fingerprint images to be taken from people instantly, are in use in 35 forces;

- we are investing £13m over two years into 10 pilot projects to test out new ways of using police staff to carry out station-based jobs traditionally performed by officers. For example, we have invested £2.5 million in new investigation teams in Surrey which will include administrators and investigative officers, allowing detective constables to do less routine paperwork and concentrate on work which is better suited to their skills, experience and training; and

- the recommendations of the new Sentencing Guidelines Council, if implemented, will reduce sentence reductions only for those who plead guilty at the courtroom door with very large potential benefits in terms of reduced file preparation where that leads to earlier guilty pleas; and

- on 1 September 2004, a Policing Bureaucracy Gateway began to operate at the Home Office and the Association of Chief Police Officers. This identifies, challenges and influences the demands made by new policies, legislation and procedures that affect the police service. We will encourage individual forces in parallel to set up their own gateways to influence the demands imposed locally.

3.20 The Government is providing practical assistance to forces in their work to reduce bureaucracy through the appointment, in January 2004, of an assistant chief constable whose responsibility is to visit forces to spread good practice, raise awareness and, where necessary, challenge existing practices. **We are setting up an actionline for officers to raise any questions they have relating to bureaucracy**. This will help to engage frontline officers in the work that is being undertaken nationally in this area. We will ensure that officers' ideas are followed up and we will publish the outcome. We have also set up an annual Reducing Bureaucracy Awards Scheme with the Police Federation, which encourages frontline officers to come up with suggestions for reducing bureaucracy. The first awards ceremony took place at the Police Federation Conference in May 2004.

3.21 Reducing bureaucracy is making an important contribution to increasing the time available for frontline duties. This is crucial in terms of getting officers out into communities. Increasing the proportion of time which police officers spend on frontline duties – a priority on which the police service has worked with us for some time – could deliver a substantial proportion of the overall 3% efficiency target set by the 2004 Spending Review settlement. Exploiting new technology, more effective deployment of officers and more effective use of police staff will also help to increase the amount of frontline policing. Other efficiency gains will be delivered through more efficient working and commercial practices. Reform of the Home Office will also help to reduce burdens on the service that can detract from efficiency. Like our overall programme itself, this is reform for a purpose – which is about helping to make policing more effective for all our communities.

3.22 The Home Office is working in partnership with the Association of Police Authorities and the Association of Chief Police Officers in a new efficiency implementation group to identify and implement the best ways to increase value for money in policing. Greater value for money will enable the service to devote the greatest possible level of resources to protecting and serving the public. Police forces and authorities are required to include in their annual policing plans efficiency plans which set out the value for money gains they intend to achieve. **We expect them, as part of their planning process, to consider what action they can take to minimise bureaucratic burdens. This is in line with the duty on police authorities to maintain an effective and efficient police force for their area.**

5.81 Looking forward, the Forensic Integration Strategy will drive and co-ordinate work to ensure that the police optimise their use of forensic science, extending our global lead on the use of DNA to all forms of forensic intelligence. The aim of the strategy is to fully integrate – by March 2008 – all forensic intelligence to provide maximum value, quality and impact in the investigative process; to enhance its value to investigators and to present more focused evidence to the Criminal Justice System. The Strategy will also support Sir Michael Bichard's recommendation for the delivery of a National Intelligence Framework.

5.82 A further key development in improving the efficiency and effectiveness of forensic science is the plan to transform the Forensic Science Service into a Public Private Partnership, via a Government owned company. This will ensure that potential for exploiting forensic science is maximised and that the police have access to the most efficient and cost-effective forensic science.

5.83 The Government is also pursuing the national roll-out to forces of a number of information and communications technologies which will ensure coherence across all forces, reduce bureaucracy and improve efficiency and effectiveness.

- **Airwave** – the new radio communication service for police forces in England, Wales and Scotland. It will be fully deployed by May 2005 and we expect all forces to be fully operational on Airwave by mid-2006.

- **Custody and Case Preparation** – provides software to give on-line guidance to police custody officers on all the procedures to be followed in the booking in of a suspect and to process cases from initiation to disposal.

- **ViSOR (Violent and Sex Offender Register)** – fulfills the joint responsibility under the Criminal Justice and Court Services Act 2001 placed on the police and probation service to register, risk assess and manage sex offenders and violent and dangerous offenders.

- **NMIS (National Management Information System)** – will provide forces with a performance management tool across all core aspects of policing and to a common data model.

Ensuring the effectiveness of policing

5.84 Finally in this Chapter, and importantly, we consider the arrangements by which those who are responsible, at whatever level, for delivering good policing, reducing crime and anti-social behaviour within communities, and responding to the needs and priorities of the public whom they serve, are held effectively to account for their performance in doing so.

5.85 The Government explored these issues in its 2003 consultation paper on police reform.[17] The approach set out in this paper to building a more responsive, citizen-focused police service – which has a deeper, stronger connection with the public – needs to be underpinned, we believe, by people having the opportunity to have a real say in how their local areas are policed. And we need to put in place stronger, clearer, more transparent ways of ensuring that those with a responsibility for ensuring that individuals and families live in safe communities are held effectively to account for their performance in carrying out those responsibilities. The Government believes this is vital for building public trust and confidence in policing. As we indicate in Chapter Two of this paper, the public is presently unclear about how things work.

5.86 The Government recognises, though, that this is a complex area. There are inextricable links, for example, to local government arrangements in England and Wales. Our 2003 consultation paper proposed looking at making improvements at three levels – neighbourhoood; district (typically covered by a Basic Command Unit/Crime and Disorder Reduction Partnership) and police force level. This approach received a general welcome. Above this level, there is also the important role which Government itself plays. It is vitally important that there are strong, transparent links between the mechanisms at all these levels.

5.87 We set out below our proposals to ensure that all communities enjoy the responsive policing they deserve. Given the complexity of some of the issues, and our desire to ensure we arrive at an arrangement which works in practice, and accommodates the different complexion of communities in different parts of the country, there are some elements of our approach which we propose to develop further. But our starting point – as set out in paragraph 5.85 above – is clear.

5.88 Proposals for arrangements at the neighbourhood level were discussed in Chapter Three (see paragraphs 3.57–3.64). Building on these proposals, the remainder of this Chapter concentrates on the district and police force level.

District level

5.89 Effective policing at the level typically covered by district or unitary councils – what are known as Basic Command Units[18] within police force areas and which often, but not always, correspond to Crime and Disorder Reduction Partnerships (CDRPs) – is crucial to ensuring community safety. This level is important not only in its own right, but because it forms a bridge between and supports activity at the very local neighbourhood level that we explored in Chapter Three and that at the police force level.

5.90 As we have made clear earlier in this paper, the Government regards effective partnership working as being vital to ensuring community safety. The creation of partnerships to tackle crime and disorder at a local level was a

---

[17] *Policing: Building safer Communities Together* – available at www.policereform.gov.uk

[18] BCUs are the main operating unit of police forces. Typically, a force will divide its territorial area into a number of BCUs, each having its own complement of officers and staff. The officer in charge of a BCU will be tasked by his or her chief constable with policing that locality and day to day decisions will be made as close to communities as possible.

fundamental feature of the Crime and Disorder Act 1998. There are now 354 Crime and Disorder Reduction Partnerships in England and 22 Community Safety Partnerships in Wales. Further details about CDRPs are contained in Appendix IV.

5.91 Many CDRPs are working well – implementing robust community safety strategies, shaped by the needs of local people and leading to tangible benefits for local communities. But a significant number of partnerships struggle to maintain a full contribution from key agencies and even successful ones are not sufficiently visible, nor we think accountable, to the public as they should be. Responses to the consultation paper, *Policing: Building Safer Communities Together*[19] indicated a broad support for CDRPs and the work of Local Strategic Partnerships.[20] But there was a general acknowledgement that further improvements were needed.

Proposals for change

5.92 Work is already underway to strengthen partnership performance. In line with our focus on the performance of police forces and Basic Command Units, the Government is currently putting in place a new performance management framework for CDRPs. This will strengthen the ability of the Home Office (working through the Government Offices for the Regions and the Welsh Assembly Government) to actively monitor partnership progress, taking action to address poor performance.

5.93 But the Government is clear that this sort of accountability must also be embedded into local communities. This means ensuring that local people know how to engage with CDRPs and understand what they can expect from the agencies working on community safety issues. To facilitate this, **the Government will formally review the partnership provisions of the Crime and Disorder Act 1998.** The Review will be conducted by the Home Office, the Local Government Association, the Association of Chief Police Officers and the Association of Police Authorities and will involve all key stakeholders and practitioners. The Review will report its conclusions by January 2005. Building on this Review **the Government proposes to publish a wider Community Safety Strategy in 2005.**

5.94 The full scope of the Crime and Disorder Act Review is set out in Appendix IV. The Government's overall objective – against which it will judge what needs to be changed in the light of the Review – is to strengthen the visibility, responsiveness to local needs and priorities, and role of local partnerships – to enable them to achieve sustained reductions in crime, disorder and substance abuse.

5.95 In meeting this objective, there are some particular areas that we want to explore further – how, for example, to embed a commitment to community safety firmly within mainstream council activity – including through the Audit Commission's Comprehensive Performance Assessment process;[21] how best to reinforce local

---

[19] Taken from *Policing: Building safer Communities Together* (Summary of Consultation Responses) pages 26-27.

[20] An LSP is a grouping of organisations and representatives of public, private, business, voluntary and community sectors, who come together to identify common objectives for their local community. A local strategic partnership normally covers a local authority area – this can be either a borough or a district, or a whole county.

[21] The Audit Commission's 2005 Comprehensive Performance Assessment (CPA) of upper tier local authorities will include community safety and engagement as elements of the overall corporate assessment.

democratic accountability for community safety through, for example, the involvement in partnerships of the district/unitary council member with an identified portfolio for community safety; and what the role of backbench council scrutiny committees might be in scrutinising the delivery of key partnership priorities. We want to look at how best to ensure the full involvement of *all* of the key local partners in committing energy and resources to joint solutions to help build safe communities. So the Review will look, specifically, at the effectiveness of the existing statutory duty on partners contained in section 17 of the Crime and Disorder Act 1998 to prevent crime and disorder – including the consequences of non-compliance with this duty.

5.96 The Government is not seeking a uniform or 'one-size-fits-all' solution for new arrangements at this 'intermediate' district level. Rather, in keeping with our overall approach to policing, we want to construct an enabling framework that works for communities across the country and facilitates local solutions to local problems.

Police Force level

5.97 At the police force level, police authorities have a statutory responsibility for ensuring that all areas have an efficient and effective police force.[22] A crucial part of this role is holding chief officers of police to account for their performance. The Government's November 2003 consultation paper on police reform explored a number of options for strengthening the current arrangements at police authority level – and the reasons why these are considered necessary. The Government was encouraged by the constructive response to its consultation exercise, particularly from the Association of Police Authorities. We remain of the view that changes need to be made to the current arrangements – we think this is vital in terms of public trust and confidence and increasing community engagement in policing.

5.98 The Government's approach is to strengthen the role of the police authority at this strategic level to ensure that communities are policed effectively, and that forces are responsive to the needs and priorities of the local public whom they serve. We also want to increase the public visibility of police authorities – which we think is best done by strengthening their ties with local government, the community itself and through the proposals in Chapter Three to require the provision of information about policing matters to be sent to all householders. To help build the closer ties and involvement in policing matters that the public wants to see, we believe that it should be the responsibility of police authorities to ensure that effective arrangements to secure public engagement are in place at the neighbourhood and district level. We explore these issues below.

Police authority membership

5.99 The Government proposes to make changes, as set out below, to strengthen the calibre, representative nature and democratic legitimacy of police authority membership.

Councillors

5.100 Strong local government input to police authority business is vital – both in terms of enabling authorities to fulfil their role and their

---

22 Police Act 1996 – section 6(1) refers.

democratic legitimacy with their communities. Councillor members of police authorities need to be closely connected to decisions about tackling crime and community safety on their councils.

5.101 **For police force areas which include unitary council areas only, the Government proposes that each council should appoint its cabinet member with responsibility for community safety to the police authority** thus ensuring stronger and more direct ties to local people and local authority services. In those police force areas which include a combination of unitary and two-tier council areas, the position is less straightforward. We will therefore discuss with our stakeholders in the police service and local government options for workable change in these areas. But we set out, in Appendix V, an illustrative example of one possible approach to two-tier areas, together with a description of what our proposed approach to unitary areas means in practice.

5.102 The governance arrangements for London's two police forces are different. The role of the Corporation of London in relation to the City of London Police is part of the unique governance arrangements for the City. We do not propose to alter them as part of these reforms. The Greater London Authority and the Metropolitan Police Authority have only been in existence since 2000. The respective roles and relationship with each other are still developing and we believe that it would be premature to change them now.

5.103 In terms of police authority size, most police authorities will retain a membership of 17. There will be no reduction in membership below this number but the maximum will not be above 21. Councillor members should still have a majority

of one. So on an authority with 17 members, 9 will be councillors; on an authority with 21 members,11 will be councillors.

5.104 The Government recognises that these proposals, by themselves, will not necessarily raise, across the board, the calibre of councillor member on police authorities or, indeed, result in authorities which are more representative of their communities than now. The success of our approach depends, in part, on the wider work which the Government is pursuing to develop strong and vibrant community leadership by local councils and councillors.

Magistrates

5.105 Magistrate members have traditionally provided an important link between the police and other parts of the criminal justice system. To ensure that this link continues but that there can also be an increase in local governance membership, **the Government proposes that there should no longer be a separate category of magistrate member on police authorities. Instead, given their experience and knowledge of the local area, where magistrate candidates apply to be independent members, there will be a presumption that at least one such magistrate will be appointed as an independent member on the authority.**

Independent members

5.106 The Government proposes to maintain the role of independent members on police authorities. But in the light of the findings of a recent Home Office review of the existing arrangements,[23] **we propose that the appointment of independent members to police authorities should be judged against a competency-**

---

23 Review of the Selection and Appointments Process of Independent Members of Police Authorities, Home Office, May 2004.

based framework of criteria, to complement the existing range of skills, knowledge and experience of other authority members. We believe that there should also be set criteria about diversity for example race, gender, age, and skills. Further detail on how we see this process working is contained in Appendix V.

Police authority chairs

5.107 The Government proposes that police authorities should continue to select their own chair by a vote of the whole authority. **But we propose that candidates for police authority chair should be subject to a competency-based selection process** overseen by an accredited assessor from the Office of the Commissioner for Public Appointments.

Police authority powers

5.108 Alongside the proposals we set out above to strengthen the membership of police authorities, the Government proposes to clarify the role which authorities play in ensuring that all communities are policed effectively. This is important for police forces and other partners with a responsibility for keeping communities safe but also, crucially, the public. Being clear about who is responsible for what in terms of policing is vital for public trust and confidence. At present, many people are very *unclear* about the position.

5.109 Some of this is about re-stating the role of police authorities. For example, police authorities have now – and will continue to have – the responsibility for setting force policing priorities. And in particular, as we have already said, holding chief officers of police to account for their performance is a crucial part of police authority business. We expect authorities to have full access and to use data and information

which will enable them to carry out this scrutiny role effectively. This includes the performance data that we have made available through iQuanta (see Appendix II) – which we expect all police authorities to use effectively – but also having full access to other information and data held by forces. But the Government believes that there are grounds for making changes to strengthen the role of police authorities in order both to underpin the approach to increasing the engagement of communities in policing and to increase the responsiveness and customer service culture of police forces across England and Wales.

5.110 The Government therefore proposes placing a duty on police authorities to:

- **take into account local policing priorities identified at Crime and Disorder Reduction Partnership (CDRP) level when developing force policing plans and strategies;**

- **oversee the relationship between CDRP and neighbourhood bodies, and ensure the implementation of citizen involvement – making sure that these arrangements are not overly bureaucratic;**

- **co-operate with neighbouring authorities to help tackle cross border crime – known as 'level two' crime – and analyse the effectiveness of their own forces' performance in doing so – the importance of which we explore in paragraphs 5.56–5.61 above;**

- **promote diversity within the police force and authority;**

- **conduct the chief constable's performance appraisal and to decide pay and bonuses – with a formal requirement to consult Her Majesty's Inspectorate of Constabulary in doing so; and**

- **request inspection by HMIC or intervention by the Police Standards Unit in respect of their force or particular parts of it where they consider this to be necessary.**

5.111 The Government will discuss, formally, the practicalities of the proposed change to the arrangements for the performance appraisal and pay of chief officers further with the Association of Chief Police Officers and the Association of Police Authorities, including what this means for training of police authority members.

5.112 The Government believes that, as now, the police authority should appoint and have the power to dismiss chief officers. But, unlike now, **we propose that it should be the chief officer of a force who should select his or her own senior management team – having consulted the police authority in drawing up a shortlist of candidates.** Under present arrangements – where appointments are made by the police authority, chief officers can be held to account for the performance of colleagues that they have had minimal influence in appointing.

5.113 In terms of the strengthened accountability role proposed for police authorities – including the responsibility for overseeing engagement at the neighbourhood and district level – the Government recognises that it is not the job of the police service to be perpetually attending meetings. **The Government's expectation is, therefore, that at the neighbourhood, Crime and Disorder Reduction Partnership**

and police force levels, accountability and scrutiny arrangements should be undertaken collaboratively to minimise off street activity by the police. Police authorities are required to include efficiency gains in their annual policing plans. As we indicate in Chapter Three, the Government expects all authorities, to minimise bureaucracy. This is particularly important in ensuring that robust accountability mechanisms are in place.

Efficiency

5.114 Police authorities are under a statutory duty to maintain an effective police force for their area – but also an efficient one. An important part of the Government's approach to making improvements in policing is the need to increase the value for money obtained from the substantially increased resources that have been provided for policing. Central to the delivery of better value for money are:

- increasing the time officers and staff spend on front line policing;

- continuing the drive to reduce bureaucracy;

- modernising the police workforce;

- increasing collaboration, or amalgamation, to deliver such corporate services as financial or human resource management; and

- buying goods and services more efficiently and effectively.

5.115 Helping the police service to achieve more for every pound spent will ensure it better meets today's policing challenges. **The Government expects this robust and positive approach to efficiency to be at the core of police authority performance, working in partnership with chief officers.**

05

Inspection and intervention

5.116 In terms of both inspection and intervention, police authorities are the focus of some limited aspects of provisions in the Local Government Act 1999. Police authorities are not, however, currently inspected on how they discharge their full responsibilities. With the clearer, strengthened role that we propose above, **the Government proposes that police authorities, like police forces, should be subject to independent inspection in order to ensure public confidence**. The Association of Police Authorities' own assessment framework could provide the components against which individual authorities might be assessed (covering, for example, community engagement; planning and performance management; resource management and corporate governance). We will explore this further as part of the Government's wider review of inspection arrangements for the criminal justice system (see paragraph 5.36) to ensure that this is activity is co-ordinated with other existing monitoring arrangements.

5.117 We think there should be some redress where this inspection or appraisal process determines that there is a serious problem with an authority. This means, we believe, broadening the type of support offered to the authority in question to match the sort of engagement available to the force. **In terms of intervention powers, the Government proposes to broaden the provisions of the Local Government Act 1999 – which already provides for some limited circumstances for intervention when authorities do not discharge, effectively, their Best Value obligations – to cover the whole range of the police authority's obligations.**

Chief officers and Government

5.118 The Government remains clear that to ensure public confidence, chief officers of police must have the freedom to exercise their proper operational responsibility for taking policing decisions. As we have already made clear in Chapter Four of this paper, the strategic vision and leadership of chief officers is vital to the success of delivering effective, more responsive policing to their communities. The Government's overall approach to, and framework for, policing is designed to ensure this is the case.

5.119 Policing must remain independent of political control and direction to retain public trust. Neither Government nor police authorities should have the right to direct a chief officer as to how they should run or conduct particular operations. But that does not mean that, as leaders of a vitally important public service in a democratic society, chief officers should not be open to proper scrutiny about those decisions and how well their force is doing in terms of reducing crime and anti-social behaviour and building safer communities. This approach has informed the proposals in this paper for strengthening the role of police authorities and community engagement in policing.

5.120 This Chapter has already explored the important role Government plays – in setting, for example, the national direction and strategic framework for policing; providing funding and powers and establishing priorities. We believe there is also a role for Government in offering support where police performance concerns require it but also – in the final reckoning – protecting the public by intervening in cases of demonstrable failure or bringing national consistency and coherence to certain policing practices where this is necessary in the public interest.

5.121 Notwithstanding the proposals in this paper to strengthen the role of police authorities, the Government believes that exceptional circumstances may still arise in which the Home Secretary may need to consider whether action should be taken in relation to the chief constable of a force in the interests of efficiency and effectiveness or for maintaining public confidence. Recent events involving the existing law (and accompanying protocol) have demonstrated the need for this process to be as simple and straightforward as possible. We intend to retain the Home Secretary's current powers, to be used in extremis, to suspend and remove chief officers. **But the Government will review the suspension process to ensure that it is as fair and straightforward as possible and discuss with the Association of Chief Police Officers, the Association of Police Authorities and the Chief Police Officers Staff Association how best to ensure there are informal as well as formal mechanisms for addressing chief officer performance issues.**

5.122 A summary of the main duties of the so-called 'tripartite' partners in policing in this country – the Home Secretary, chief officers and police authorities – is contained in Appendix VI.

Chapter Six: Summary of proposals

Chapter Six – Summary of proposals

Proposal	Paragraph Reference
Chapter 3 – A New Relationship between the Police and the Public – Building trust and Confidence	
In supporting neighbourhood policing: • joint guidance will be set out on neighbourhood policing for forces with the Association of Chief Police Officers and the National Centre for Policing Excellence early in 2005. • a programme will be put in place to help forces implement neighbourhood policing and make sure that the highly skilled role of neighbourhood officer is recognised, valued and trained in the same way as other specialists within the police service. • the roll-out of neighbourhood policing will be supported with substantial investment through the new Neighbourhood Policing Fund. We will deliver 25,000 community support officers and wardens by 2008. • a national community policing TOGETHER Academy programme will be run in March 2005 to ensure police officers and their CSO colleagues have the tools, the know-how and the backing to tackle anti-social behaviour in the communities they serve.	3.16
We are setting up an actionline for officers to raise any questions they have relating to bureaucracy	3.20
We expect police authorities and forces, as part of their planning process to consider what action they can take to minimise bureaucratic burdens.	3.22
Every force will have national standards of service in place by the end of 2006 and will agree in a 'Contract' with their communities how these can be built on locally, to reflect the particular needs of the communities they serve.	3.29
The success of the Together Action Line will be built on to provide a direct single non-emergency number for the public which will deal with non-emergency issues of policing, crime and anti-social behaviour.	3.36

Proposal	Paragraph Reference
To improve the responsiveness and customer service culture across all police forces, a number of projects will be brought together in 2005 as part of a national strategy to improve call handling: • the Association of Chief Police Officers' programme of work to bring all forces up to the same high standard of call handling, which is due to complete in April 2005; • a thematic inspection on contact management to be carried out during 2005 by Her Majesty's Inspectorate of Constabulary (HMIC); and • a manual of best practice on the most effective ways to manage calls from the public which will be published following HMICs inspection.	3.41
From April 2005, the comparative assessment of overall force performance will include the satisfaction of victims of crime about how easy it was to make contact with the police, how they were treated by staff, the actions police officers took and how they were kept informed of progress.	3.43
Greater emphasis will be given to assessing customer service and responsiveness as part of the changes to overall arrangements for inspection and accountability.	3.44
A statutory minimum requirement will be introduced in terms of what each household can expect to receive in terms of local policing information.	3.51
New forms of support and advice will be made available on how frontline staff can engage more effectively with local communities.	3.54
Changes will be made to the way police performance is measured and inspected so that it reflects the priorities of the public and their views about the policing they have received.	3.56
A joint duty will be placed on the police and local authorities in each CDRP area to ensure they have sufficient arrangements in place to deliver a range of engagement opportunities for local neighbourhoods and to respond to concerns that are raised as a result.	3.59

06

Proposal	Paragraph Reference
The following changes will be made to existing statutory arrangements: • extension of the responsibility on police authorities to secure the implementation of a strategy to engage the community at all levels – including neighbourhoods – within the police area; • a direct responsibility on the police in partnership with other bodies to put the strategy into place and to have arrangements to respond to neighbourhood level concerns; and • a requirement for CDRPs to oversee the delivery of neighbourhood level priorities agreed with local communities. This may involve the routine establishment of joint tasking and co-ordination groups that are already in place in some areas.	3.59
The Home Office will work with the Office of the Deputy Prime Minister as part of the governments' local government strategy, to develop a range of ways in which ward councillors can be assisted to act as advocates.	3.66
We will introduce a specific mechanism for triggering action.	3.69
The challenge remains how to effectively "empower" BCU commanders while maintaining the coherence of the force and avoiding the creation of uneconomical units. The Government proposes to: • carefully examine the precise role of BCU commanders and their contribution to partnership working. This will take into account the different contexts of policing across the country and address the balance of activities between those that are delegated and those that are better managed centrally; and • develop further the key enablers of delegation to BCU Commanders. We will examine the importance of leadership, looking particularly at how far the direction and corporate vision which chief constables provide and the trust they exhibit in their commanders are essential for successful delegation to occur, and how this needs to be supported by appropriate training for all senior ranks. We will examine the use of stronger mechanisms for BCU commanders to be held accountable for their performance, and investigate the relationships between force HQs and BCUs, including how resources are to be balanced and negotiated between them to provide a clear operating framework.	3.85
Clear guidance on a BCU delegation and empowerment will be produced:	3.86

Proposal	Paragraph Reference
Chapter 4 – Building a New Workforce	
The Core Leadership Development Programme will ensure that officers of all levels, including post probationary constables, can develop the important leadership skills that will benefit and inform the way police constables and community support officers work together in serving the community.	4.12
Mechanisms will be put in place for continuously developing constables' operational skills.	4.14
Officers will no longer be required to have spent a specific number of years in a particular rank before being eligible for promotion.	4.15
Sergeants, inspectors and chief inspectors – and police staff at equivalent levels – will all have access to the Core Leadership Development Programme, which will aim to develop their managerial, leadership and some operational skills.	4.18
The national performance and development scheme will be revised to give police authorities a leading role in operating it.	4.22
In preparation for the growth in CSO numbers: • a minimum set of powers will be developed, on the basis of experience so far, which all CSOs need to possess to play a full part in neighbourhood policing. This will include enforcement powers such as the power to require a name and address, the power to confiscate alcohol and powers to issue fixed penalty notices; • forces will be empowered to be able to grant the power of detention to CSOs; • the Government will work with forces and Skills for Justice to develop role profiles linked to the national occupational standards. This will enable forces to match recruitment, training and development programmes to the work that CSOs perform; • national recruitment of CSOs will be developed. This will take into account pilots developed by the Metropolitan Police and others;	4.29

Proposal	Paragraph Reference
• training packages for higher education colleges will be created for those who have yet to join the service, and national induction and training packages for local delivery by forces. We will also ensure we reach all CSOs and their key police colleagues through a national TOGETHER Academy Programme – to ensure they have the tools, know how and backing to tackle anti social behaviour in the communities they serve. • support training will be provided for supervisors of CSOs, who may be members of police staff or constables as well as sergeants; • the terms and conditions negotiated in the Police Staff Council will provide the right rewards to recruit, retain and motivate CSOs and give forces the flexibilities they need to maximise the benefits from deploying them; • consideration will be given to how best to enhance the career structure for CSOs so the best can advance without necessarily becoming uniformed officers; • commitment to national and local evaluation and encouragement of the sharing of expertise and good practice across the police service will be maintained.	
Consideration will be given to how to develop similar arrangements for police staff to those already available to police officers under the High Potential Development Scheme which was introduced in 2002 to support and develop future senior police leaders.	4.32
The roles of police authorities and chief officers in the appointment of members of police staff of ACPO equivalent rank should be the same as those for senior officer appointments.	4.33
Any regulatory bar which prevents members of police staff from carrying out functions appropriate to their role as senior managers will be removed.	4.34
The necessary regulatory changes will be proposed in the Police Negotiating Board to enable forces to run separate exercises for police staff to become officers, in accordance with the National Recruitment Standard, and to appoint successful candidates as soon as there are vacancies.	4.36
It will be proposed in the Police Staff Council to review how more effective career structures for police staff might be put in place.	4.37

Proposal	Paragraph Reference
We will work with stakeholders to increase the number of and effectiveness of police service volunteers: • identify and share good practice in the recruitment, management, training and deployment of volunteers; • encourage the use of dedicated staff to support the implementation of good practice. We have already awarded funding of up to £70,000 per force in England and Wales for initiatives to help increase numbers and ensure special constables are well managed and purposefully deployed; • develop role profiles and a training programme based on national occupational standards for members of the wider policing family, including special constables and police support volunteers; • support recruitment and marketing efforts to better publicise police service volunteering roles and the personal development opportunities they give to local people and community groups; • investigate wider roles and specialist uses of volunteers; and • help forces to establish partnerships with businesses, encouraging businesses to support staff who volunteer with forces, in recognition of their added training and skills.	4.40
Career pathways will defined and the take-up promoted.	4.45
Consideration will be given to developing professional registers for the police service, in line with practice in other professions.	4.45
A formal qualifications framework for the service will be developed – built on work-based assessment against national occupational standards. There will be qualifications for all areas of policing, including operational activities such as investigations and other activities such as management.	4.45
Aspects of the current High Potential Development scheme will be reviewed to see if there are changes which should be made.	4.47
Proposals will be introduced in the Police Advisory Board to make recruitment as a police officer dependent on completion of the procedures set out in the NRS.	4.48

06

Proposal	Paragraph Reference
Multiple points of entry to the police service will be introduced, removing the requirement that all police officers serve specific amounts of time at junior ranks before being promoted to more senior ranks.	4.49
There will be a review of whether the offer which the police service is able to make currently to graduates is sufficiently attractive. This will be looked at particularly in relation to opportunities for accelerated career development and whether more can be done to market police careers more effectively, and on a national basis, to the graduate recruitment market.	4.51
A single national qualification for officers who successfully complete their probation will be introduced.	4.54
Work will be taken forward with further and higher education establishments to enable people with an interest in policing to undergo relevant training before actually joining a particular force and beginning their careers.	4.54
The PDR scheme will be overhauled with the aim of making it clearer, more robust and easier to use. The Police Performance Assessment Framework (PPAF) will be used to monitor the use of PDRs by forces.	4.57
Work-based assessment will be extended throughout the service as an alternative to the existing examinations.	4.58
Enhanced training will be developed leading to a specialist qualification for people wishing to take on BCU commander roles.	4.60
A mandatory qualification for superintendents seeking to become BCU commanders should be developed over time.	4.60
The way in which the service identifies senior talent will be strengthened. The Senior Careers Advisory Service (SCAS) will be aimed at chief officers and superintendents with the potential to become chief officers, and their equivalents among senior police staff.	4.61
Proposals have been made to the Police Advisory Board to make changes in regulations and determinations so that a member of a police force shall not belong to the BNP, Combat 18 or the National Front or any other organisation whose constitution, aims, objectives or pronouncements are incompatible with the duty imposed by section 71 of the Race Relations Act 1976.	4.75

Proposal	Paragraph Reference
Standards for language skills other than in English will be developed so that forces may take the obvious advantage of taking those skills into account in recruiting where this is operationally justified. Such candidates will of course need to meet the other elements of the national recruitment standard.	4.78
A national panel of assessors will be established from ethnic minority communities and include a regulatory requirement in National Recruitment Standards that all assessment and selection panels include representatives from ethnic minority communities and that where insufficient local assessors are available, members of the national panel take part in the assessment centres.	4.78
A standard exit interview procedure will be introduced to help us understand why people are leaving the service, particularly in the first six months (where ethnic minority recruits are disproportionately represented).	4.78
The Government will work with the National Black Police Association (NBPA) in support of its development plan and strengthen the support network for ethnic minority officers.	4.78
Specific exercises will be run to encourage members of ethnic minorities with successful careers in other professions to apply for lateral entry to senior ranks in the service. They will of course be required to meet the same standards for entry as majority community candidates.	4.78
Promotion and progression procedures will be reviewed to ensure they are fair, transparent and have no adverse impact on any group.	4.78
Barriers to the recruitment of women will be reviewed. Wherever possible, police training, including foundation and probationer training, will be made non-residential and available on a part-time basis. Family-friendly, flexible working patterns should be available as a matter of course.	4.81
The stages of the promotion process will be examined to identify barriers to progression of women and take steps to remove them. In particular, examination will be given to what is needed to improve support and progression for ethnic minority women officers.	4.81
The service will be consulted on the introduction of challenging progression targets to ensure greater representation of women at higher levels of the service and on the High Potential Development scheme.	4.81

06

Proposal	Paragraph Reference
A strategy will be published for using learning and development to improve police performance in race and diversity over the next five years.	4.82
A new duty will be placed on police authorities to promote diversity within the police force and authority.	4.84
The Government will explore with the staff associations and unions, and with the Independent chair of the PAB and PNB how to formalise the relationship between police staff unions and the PAB.	4.86
Proposals will be developed for change in deployment arrangements in consultation with the police service, including the staff associations and trade unions.	4.88
More stretching targets will be introduced to build on the improvements already delivered on police sickness absence.	4.89
Forces will be encouraged to assess people management skills in performance and Development Review (PDRs) at all levels; develop a competency framework for HR managers; and improve access to professional training for HR specialists.	4.91
PPAF measures will be developed to reflect a broader range of HR activities – in particular the effectiveness of force PDR systems – and HMIC will continue to refine its baseline assessment activity in this area.	4.92
Chapter 5 – Ensuring Effectiveness	
The forthcoming National Policing Plan will complement the approach set out in this paper and will be more strategic and concise than previous Plans.	5.8
In light of the Bichard report the government is committed to: • introducing a statutory Code of Practice on police information management by the end of 2004; • introducing a national IT system for handling and sharing police intelligence by 2007; • overhauling existing vetting procedures; • developing more integrated and consistent arrangements for checking the suitability of those wishing to work with children.	5.12

Proposal	Paragraph Reference
A new Code of Practice will be introduced to ensure NIM is used as effectively as possible and that the legal framework within which it must be applied is understood by all.	5.19
A single overall grading for each police force in England and Wales will be published.	5.25
Forces graded 'excellent', will have a general 'inspection break', for rolling 12-month periods.	5.28
Forces graded 'excellent' will benefit from additional funding and freedoms on targets.	5.29
The existing statutory powers to take remedial action where police forces or Basic Command Units are underperforming will be revised. The collaborative engagement and improvement process will be put on a statutory footing; with powers of compulsion (i.e. intervention) arising only where sufficient improvement fails to transpire.	5.32
As part of the process for amending the way the intervention power works, the Government proposes to revise the trigger to bring it more into line with the wider set of information sources – other than HMIC inspection *alone* – which now inform our views of police force performance.	5.34
As part of a general review of the inspection arrangements for public services, the Government therefore intends to consult early in the New Year on different, more coherent arrangements for the end-to-end inspection of the Criminal Justice System.	5.38
A National Policing Improvement Agency will be created.	5.42
Consideration will be given to the creation of dedicated teams across regions or groups of forces with the specific task of co-ordinating the effort against level two criminality in that region or area.	5.59
A duty will be placed on police authorities to co-operate with neighbouring authorities to help tackle cross border crime and to analyse the effectiveness of their forces in this area of activity.	5.61
The Home Secretary has commissioned Her Majesty's Inspectorate of Constabulary (HMIC) to take an in-depth look at the issue of force structures in England and Wales.	5.63

Proposal	Paragraph Reference
Consideration will be given to further development of arrangements for lead forces or specialisms, in particular for those crimes which, by their very nature, are not confined to geographical force areas – such as hi-tech crime or online paedophilia.	5.66
The partnership provisions of the Crime and Disorder Act 1998 will be formally reviewed.	5.93
Building on the review of the Crime and Disorder Act 1998, a wider community safety strategy will be published in 2005.	5.93
In force areas which include unitary council areas only, each council should appoint its cabinet member with the responsibility for community safety to the police authority.	5.101
There will no longer be a separate category of magistrate member on police authorities. Instead, given their experience and knowledge of the local area, where magistrate candidates apply to be independent members, there will be a presumption that at least one such magistrate will be appointed as an independent member on the authority.	5.105
The appointment of independent members to police authorities should be made on merit and ability, judged against a competency-based framework of criteria.	5.106
Candidates for police authority chair should be subject to a competency-based selection process.	5.107
A duty will be placed on police authorities to: • take into account local policing priorities identified at Crime and Disorder Reduction Partnership (CDRP) level when publishing force policing plans and strategies; • oversee the relationship between CDRPs and neighbourhood bodies and ensure the implementation of citizen involvement – making sure that these arrangements are not overly bureaucratic; • co-operate with neighbouring authorities to help tackle cross border crime – known as 'level 2' crime – and analyse the effectiveness of their own forces' performance in doing so; • promote diversity within the police force and authority; • conduct the chief constable's performance appraisal and to decide pay and bonuses-with a requirement to consult Her Majesty's Inspectorate of Constabulary (HMIC) in doing so.	5.110

Proposal	Paragraph Reference
• request inspection by HMIC or intervention by the Police Standards Unit in respect of their force or particular parts of it where they consider this to be necessary.	
Police authorities will be given the power to request inspection by HMIC or intervention by the Police Standards Unit in respect of their force or particular parts of it.	5.110
The chief officer of a force should select his or her own senior management team – having consulted the police authority in drawing up a shortlist of candidates.	5.112
Accountability arrangements at neighbourhood, CDRP and force level should be undertaken collaboratively to minimise off-street activity by the police.	5.113
A robust and positive approach to efficiency to be at the core of police authority performance.	5.115
Police authorities, like police forces, should be subject to independent inspection in order to ensure public confidence.	5.116
In terms of intervention powers the provisions of the Local Government Act 1999 Act will be broadened to cover the whole range of the police authority's obligations.	5.117
The suspension process for chief officers will be reviewed to ensure that it is as fair and straightforward as possible. Discussions will be held with the Association of Chief Police Officers, Association of Police Authorities and the Chief Police Officers Staff Association on how best to ensure there are informal as well as formal mechanisms for addressing chief officer performance issues.	5.121

06

Appendices

Appendix I: Public Service Reform

i. The Government recognises that policing is, in some respects, necessarily different to other public services. But the debate around further reform of policing needs, nonetheless, to be seen within the important context of the Government's wider strategy on public service reform. The Prime Minister has set out four principles of public service reform, to deliver services better designed around the needs of their customers – namely, national standards, devolution and delegation, flexibility and expanding choice.[1] Clearly, with the police service, there are some specific additional principles which are of critical importance, such as the engagement of communities and a commitment to partnership working, which are equally as fundamental as the four principles listed above. Our programme of police reform, like the Government's wider agenda of public service reform, will build on all of these key principles in order to deliver improvements.

ii. There is also an important read across between policing and other public services, particularly the wider Criminal Justice System, local government, transport, health, education and children's services.

Criminal Justice Reform

iii. Together, the police and the other agencies that make up the Criminal Justice System (CJS) deliver one of the major public services in the country. Strong criminal justice has a crucial role to play in reducing crime and anti-social behaviour and making people feel safer.

iv. We have already made a great deal of progress in making the CJS more effective and this is borne out by our results. 7% more offences were brought to justice between March 2002 and March 2004, while public confidence in the system, which had been declining, has increased by 3% in the past twelve months. But we want to achieve more. The Home Office, the Department for Constitutional Affairs and the Office of the Attorney General published a five-year strategic plan for the CJS[2] in July 2004 which set out further reform for our criminal justice services to make sure that we have a modern and efficient system, which is visible and responsive to the law-abiding citizen.

v. To show what reform will have been achieved in five years' time, we have devised the following vision, which describes the delivery of justice in 2008:

---

[1] The Prime Minister's 4 principles of public service reform are: 1) **national standards** that really matter to the public, within a framework of clear accountability, designed to ensure that citizens have the right to high quality services wherever they live; 2) **devolution and delegation** to the front line, giving local leaders responsibility and accountability for delivery, and the opportunity to design and develop services around the needs of local people; 3) **flexibility** for public service organisations and their staff to achieve the diversity of service provision needed to respond to the wide range of customer aspirations; and 4) **expanding choice** for the customer, helping to ensure that services are designed around their customers with an element of contestability between alternative suppliers.

[2] *Cutting Crime, Delivering Justice*, published July 2004.

- the public will have confidence that the CJS is effective and serves all communities fairly;

- victims and witnesses will receive a consistent high standard of service from all criminal justice agencies;

- more offences will be brought to justice through a modern and efficient justice process;

- rigorous enforcement will revolutionise compliance with sentences and orders of the court; and

- criminal justice will be a joined up, modern and well-run service, and an excellent place to work for people of all backgrounds.

vi. If people believe that the CJS is capable of responding swiftly and effectively when a crime has been committed, this will help to reassure the public and reduce the fear of crime. Improving basic service performance is crucial to building public confidence that the CJS is effective. But it is also vital that the system communicates better with staff, users and the public, introduces consistently high service standards across CJS agencies, and responds demonstrably to community concerns.

vii. We plan to improve communications so that the public has a clear understanding of the CJS and how it is being reformed. Staff have a key advocacy role to play, so we will engage them in this task. And we are pioneering ways of improving community engagement. For example, we are introducing specialist court hearings on anti-social behaviour, domestic violence and drugs to respond better to problems in local areas and provide a targeted approach to offending, while the Community Justice Centre pilot in North Liverpool will trial a community-based response to tackling low-level crime and anti-social behaviour and their causes.

Community justice in Liverpool

The Liverpool Community Justice Centre is based on the philosophy behind the Red Hook Community Justice Centre in New York, using a problem solving approach to tackle local priorities.

The Community Justice Centre, which will be operational by the end of 2004, will tackle the quality of life crimes and anti-social behaviour issues that can blight communal life. It will act as a focus for the community, with the multi-purpose building bringing services and facilities to local people. Within the building, there will be a courtroom, plus services which are available to help tackle offending, such as drug counselling, debt and housing advice, and basic education skills. Services within the centre will not just be offered to offenders but to any member of the community on a walk-in basis.

The local community has been involved in the development of the Centre and will be involved in its operation through a volunteer force and community advisory panels. Close partnership with the police will ensure that local police priorities and the way cases are handled in the Centre reflect genuine community priorities.

The pilot marks an innovative departure in the delivery of justice, providing an opportunity to respond to community priorities and to have a positive and tangible effect on people's everyday lives.

viii. Raising customer service standards across the system is important. But we need to devote particular time and resources to improving the way victims and witnesses are treated. Although the chance of becoming a victim of crime is now at its lowest for twenty years, the treatment of victims and witnesses often falls well short of what they should be able to expect.

ix. To address this, we are introducing a statutory Victims Code of Practice. This will set out the minimum standards of service that victims can expect. But to galvanise action to improve services and focus criminal justice agencies on particular areas which need attention, we have identified seven national priorities. These are:

- victims and witnesses are given information about services and about their cases;

- victims and witnesses receive a consistently high quality service from CJS staff;

- victims and witnesses who require emotional or practical help are offered the relevant services;

- victims' views are sought and used throughout the CJS process;

- the needs of vulnerable and intimidated witnesses are identified and met; and intimidation is tackled;

- the experience of victims and witnesses going to court is improved; and

- the needs of victims of domestic violence are met and repeat victimisation is tackled.

x. Delivering these priorities will make a radical difference to the experience of victims and witnesses, in turn building public confidence in the system, and making witnesses more willing to participate in the criminal justice process again.

xi. Public agencies also need to acknowledge and understand that being a victim of anti-social behaviour is a different experience to being a victim of other types of crime. Tackling, not tolerating, anti-social behaviour is about confronting unacceptable behaviour. This can be difficult, especially when problems in communities are longstanding. Concerns about intimidation and reprisals can act as a powerful disincentive for people to report incidents, leaving problem behaviour unchecked and making it difficult for the police and local authorities to tackle anti-social behaviour effectively. To address this, the Government recently announced a series of new measures aimed at helping victims of anti-social behaviour. These include measures to tackle intimidation of victims and witnesses and an expansion of the number of anti-social behaviour courts by more than three-fold from twelve to forty-one.

xii. Our key goal is to reduce crime. And when a crime is committed, the public has a right to expect that the CJS will do all it can to bring the perpetrator to justice. This requires high quality policing to detect the crime; close Crown Prosecution Service (CPS) and police co-operation as the 'prosecution team' to ensure that the right charge is made and that robust cases are brought to court; proper care, protection and support for victims and other witnesses; and collaborative working by criminal justice agencies to make sure that the trial goes ahead on the scheduled day.

xiii. In order to bring more offences to justice, we are making changes at every stage of the criminal justice process:

- the Fixed Penalty Notice Scheme will be extended to a wider range of low level offences which the police can deal with as effectively outside court; and the use of conditional cautioning is also being piloted;

- improving technology and the spread of good practice will help the police to raise detection rates;

- by March 2007, the CPS will support every police force by providing 24 hour advice seven days a week on their investigations and will determine the charges. This will result in more defendants pleading guilty earlier in the process and better prepared cases for trial;

- through the Effective Trial Management Scheme, we will make sure that where cases do need to come to trial, they arrive at court ready to proceed, reducing the numbers of wasted trial hearings by a fifth and in the magistrates' courts by a third by 2008;

- new police-CPS Witness Care Units will operate in all areas by the end of 2005 to support witnesses as their cases progress, in order to raise witness attendance at court and cut the number of cases which collapse because the witness has not turned up.

xiv. Ensuring that the decisions and orders of the court are carried out swiftly is a key test of the effectiveness of the CJS and a key driver of successful CJS performance in bringing offences to justice and maintaining public confidence. First time compliance is our primary goal, but when defendants and offenders do not co-operate, we need to take robust enforcement action.

xv. We will improve enforcement performance across the board year on year – increasing defendant attendance and ensuring the swift execution of warrants; increasing the percentage of fines collected; bringing community penalty breaches to court more quickly; and recovering more assets. We will do this by making sure that people on the frontline have the right powers, tools and information to deliver, and by providing financial incentives to improving performance.

xvi. We will not achieve our vision for the delivery of justice without effective partnership working between the police and other CJS agencies, backed by modern technology. Collaborative working at both a national and local level is beginning to be embedded firmly across the CJS. At a national level, the creation of the National Criminal Justice Board, on which Ministers from the three CJS departments – the Home Office, the Department for Constitutional Affairs and the Office of the Attorney General – plus heads of the criminal justice agencies, the Association of Police Authorities and the Association of Chief Police Officers, and the judiciary are represented, has provided strengthened leadership. The establishment of the Office for Criminal Justice Reform, a cross-departmental team that supports all CJS agencies in working together to provide an improved service to the public, has given joint working a further boost. And at local level, Local Criminal Justice Boards, set up in April 2003 to bring together the heads of criminal justice agencies to work in partnership, have got off to an excellent start.

xvii. An unparalleled investment in modern technology for the criminal justice system will also help to make this vision a reality. By 2008, the £2 billion invested in IT will have transformed IT infrastructure and systems, increasing efficiency and effectiveness. For the first time, all criminal justice professionals will have access to standard office applications, such as email, there will be national systems for managing cases for each criminal justice agency, and these case management systems will be linked so that information can be shared between agencies, speeding up key processes and improving data quality.

Local Government

xviii. Local government has a key role in providing strong and visible leadership to communities and working to join up services to meet local needs and priorities. Councils act as champions for their local area, promoting the well-being of the community as a whole and providing a clear line of democratic accountability between decision-makers and the people they serve. There has been substantial progress in developing this role in recent years. To build on this, the Deputy Prime Minister recently launched a debate on the future of local government,[3] which has clear and important implications for many areas of the Government's work, particularly community safety. The debate will focus on how local government can harness its role to deliver better outcomes for people and places through working more effectively with partners at local, regional and national level. Key themes include developing strong and vibrant community leadership, improving citizen engagement and participation, and improving service delivery and performance – all of which are integral to the Government's vision for police reform.

xix. Local authorities are particularly well placed to have an impact on the social, economic and environmental causes of crime through the community-based services they provide. Through education, social care, youth, leisure, transport, housing, environmental and other services, councils can and do work effectively to prevent crime, anti-social behaviour and substance misuse. As a result of good quality planning, design and street lighting, for example, local authorities can help to reduce crime and disorder and the fear of crime. Through effective management of the night time economy, they can make a significant contribution to reducing levels of alcohol-related crime and disorder in town and city centres, as well as playing a key role in reducing other forms of anti-social behaviour such as begging and nuisance neighbours. And through enforcement of licensing and other regulations they can help reduce alcohol and drug-related crime, and help to ensure that alcohol and substance misusers and their families receive treatment and support. The Licensing Act 2003 transfers licensing powers to new licensing authorities, which are generally local authorities. From November 2005, when the old licensing laws end and the new laws begin, they will have an important role to play in the prevention of crime and disorder.

Environmental crime

Anti-social behaviour includes litter, fly-tipping, graffiti, fly-posting, dog-fouling and other problems that impact on the physical environment. These kind of problems degrade public spaces, are the subject of many complaints made by the public and can be significant criminal offences. Enviro-crimes can also make people feel afraid. In addition, when these problems are allowed to take over an area, other forms of anti-social behaviour may proliferate. Abandoned and other 'nuisance' vehicles in particular have a negative effect on the quality of the local environment. They can attract vandalism, rubbish and arson and can be the result of, or the means to commit, a crime.

---

[3] *The future of local government: Developing a 10 year vision*, published 27 July 2004

Environmental crime *(cont)*

Tackling environmental problems produces tangible results. That is why the Government is committed to work in this area, complementing the Cleaner, Safer, Greener Strategy. Moreover, the benefits of action against environmental anti-social behaviour go beyond keeping streets and estates clean and free from graffiti and other enviro-crime problems. Action of this nature can help to build confidence in the effectiveness of public services.

xx. Central to the effectiveness of local government is partnership working. This is at its most effective when local authorities encourage Crime and Disorder Reduction Partnerships, Drug Action Teams and Local Strategic Partnerships to work more closely together and ensure that the greatest impact of their community safety effort is in local areas of greatest need. The Home Office Crime Reduction Programme helps the most vulnerable members of communities through identifying, developing and promulgating good practice on a range of interventions, including target hardening. The 42% reduction in burglary since 1997 is a good example of target hardening helping to bring about reductions in crime, while car park strategies have contributed to a fall in vehicle theft. This approach has been most successful when combined with initiatives which also educate communities on the steps they can take to help themselves. Businesses too have a key role to play here – which is why the Government has facilitated joint business/local authority work to make improvements to the quality of their local environments through the creation of Business Improvement Districts. The

Home Office is due to publish a summary of the Commercial Victimisation Study at the end of 2004, which will provide useful information on levels of commercial crime.

xxi. A further critical area of partnership working relates to children and young people. It is vital that all agencies that deliver services for children and young people work effectively together in order to reduce young people's involvement in crime and substance misuse. Local authorities work with children and young people at risk, undertake targeted work with persistent truants and excluded pupils to prevent them falling into criminal activity and provide leisure activities to help bring down levels of anti-social behaviour. Organisations such as Connexions, Sure Start and Youth Inclusion Programmes have a critical role to play. Close partnership working will be further facilitated by the reforms to children and young people's services following the Green Paper, *Every Child Matters*. These reforms are considered further in the section below on education and children's services.

Transport

xxii. One of the Government's aims is for a safe and secure transport system. Crime and the fear of crime whilst walking to, waiting for and travelling on public transport can restrict people accessing local services, particularly in socially excluded areas. Partnership working is essential in tackling crime and fear of crime across the whole transport journey. Tackling transport crime can also lead to the apprehension of offenders of other crimes. For example, in London the Transport Operational Command Unit is a partnership between Transport for London and the Metropolitan Police. Revenue Protection Inspectors board buses to inspect tickets. If a passenger fails to produce a ticket and refuses to give their name and address, the police are called and the passenger is taken to a police station for fingerprinting and searching. In the course of 7.5 million passenger checks in 2003-04, over 13,500 penalty fares and 35,000 notices for prosecution were issued, including for theft, deception, handling stolen goods, disorderly behaviour and drug offences.

Health

xxiii. In March 2004, the Secretary of State for Health launched a consultation on the strategy for improving health and the provision of health services.[4] The consultation sought views on how a real difference could be made to people's lives by promoting a healthy lifestyle for all. The aim was to ensure the appropriate local environment, services, facilities and information to enable citizens to choose a healthy lifestyle. There is a clear link between the health and community safety agendas, with crime clearly impacting negatively on health, in particular on mental health. Citizens need the confidence of a safe and crime-free environment in which they can access the services and facilities that they need to stay healthy. We, as Government, must join up our efforts to improve the all-round environment and quality of life available to citizens so that they in turn can take personal responsibility for their health.

xxiv. There is also a strong link with health in relation to drug and alcohol treatment. This partnership of interest has been underpinned by the fact that since April 2004, Primary Care Trusts in England and health authorities in Wales have been formal members of Crime and Disorder Reduction Partnerships. Their new status as full partners within the partnerships is enabling health trusts and practitioners to have real influence in shaping local action to tackle crime, drug and alcohol misuse and the causes of crime.

Education and children's services

xxv. The provision of education and children's services is also crucial to the success of the Government's wider vision of public service reform and to the safety of our communities. The Secretary of State for Education and Skills published, in July 2004, his Department's five year strategy for children and learners.[5] The themes running through that strategy accord with those outlined in this policy paper. The vision is of a system which is tailored to the needs of the user and local priorities, with flexibility for those at the front line to demonstrate leadership and deliver excellence. Above all, the aim is to have local services working in effective and successful partnerships, with local accountability, community regeneration and high standards for those who need and use these services.

---

[4] *Choosing Health? A consultation on improving people's health*, published 3 March 2004

[5] Available at www.teachernet.gov.uk/wholeschool/extendedschools/News/fiveyearstrategy

xxvi. The police service already has an important role in working with young people in schools and the wider community. The Department for Education and Skills, Association of Chief Police Officers and the Youth Justice Board jointly lead Safer Schools Partnerships, where police work in partnership with pupils, school staff and the wider community to provide a safe and secure school community, ensure that young people remain in education, challenge unacceptable behaviour and reduce the prevalence of crime and victimisation amongst young people. By working with young people to prevent crime and disorder at an early age, police officers can develop good relationships which extend outside the school gates and into local communities. There are currently over 400 schools with Safer Schools Partnership police officers.

xxvii. Children's services are undergoing a major programme of whole-system change that will be particularly relevant to the police. The Children Bill, which is currently before Parliament, provides for a duty to be placed on the police and other local agencies to co-operate with the local authority and its partners in making arrangements to improve the wellbeing of all children. The intention is for this to come into effect from April 2005, with the aim of improving these outcomes for children and young people by the different agencies, whose work impacts on children, young people and their families, working together to address the needs of each child or young person in an integrated way.

xxviii. The duty to co-operate underpins the move towards Children's Trusts. Thirty-five Pathfinder Authorities are already piloting trust arrangements, which will mean more professionals working together in effective multi-disciplinary teams to tackle cultural and professional divides. The duty to have regard to the need to safeguard and promote children's welfare placed on the police and other agencies is an important step in ensuring that all agencies play their roles individually and collectively in safeguarding children from harm. This integrated front line working relies upon effective partnership working of all providers of services for children and young people, for example health, education, social services, youth services, Connexions, Sure Start, Youth Offending Teams and Drug Action Teams. Children's Trusts will provide a mechanism for partnership working, needs analysis, joint planning and commissioning of services and accountability arrangements that make integrated front-line delivery possible.

Appendix II: Police Performance

Assessing performance – data

i. Police performance in England and Wales is assessed by what is known as the Policing Performance Assessment Framework (PPAF) – which measures performance against seven key areas. One area focuses on force performance against local priorities, while the other six focus on reducing crime; investigating crime; citizen-focus; promoting public safety; providing assistance; and the use of resources. In keeping with the approach to policing outlined in this policy paper, improvement in all these areas is crucial to delivering greater public satisfaction and better trust and confidence in policing across all communities.

ii. Information is also managed in a new way on a system called iQuanta, which provides police forces, police authorities and local partnerships with real-time and, critically, comparative, up to the minute information on the performance of all forces, the Basic Command Units (BCUs) within them and the 354 Crime and Disorder Reduction Partnerships in England and the 22 Community Safety Partnerships in Wales.

iii. This focus on performance has changed the way in which forces operate very much for the better. At local (BCU) level, BCUs use real-time data and the National Intelligence Model methods to analyse crime trends in their area, to understand who their prolific offenders are, and local concerns, and to prioritise accordingly. BCU commanders and heads of support branches are then held to account at the police force level by its leadership as part of a regular and effective review of the performance of the force. This is complemented by the role of the police authority, which is responsible for ensuring that the chief officers of the force are delivering on the priorities of the local policing plan.

iv. Thanks to iQuanta and the work of the Police Standards Unit, a force is now able to see its position relative to other comparable forces and BCUs within them. And finally, at a national level, the Police Standards Unit is able to take an overview – comparing forces and BCUs across the country and highlighting where performance is good, and where it isn't. When performance falls short, the Police Standards Unit can then work with the forces and BCUs concerned to ensure practical help is given to make improvements.

Police Performance Management Guide

The Police Standards Unit Performance Management Guide sets out what a force needs to be doing if it is to be well-organised and able to drive and sustain high standards of performance. The 10 hallmarks are:

- Clarity about the roles and responsibilities of the police authority, chief constable and managers – at all levels – for performance

- A framework which links performance to corporate planning, budgeting and resource management

- Chief constable ownership and active involvement in the force's performance review process

- Performance review structures which hold staff to account, replicated from top to bottom and across operational and support departments

- Recognition of good performance but with a relentless follow-up where performance falls short

- A culture of continuous improvement evident throughout the organisation

- Clearly articulated priorities which are widely understood by officers and police staff at every level of the force

- Individual Performance and Development Review objectives and appraisal linked directly to performance

- Timely, accurate and relevant data to inform decision-making

- Performance data is easily captured and clearly reported

Role of Her Majesty's Inspectorate of Constabulary (HMIC)

v. The Government recognises that performance is not just about figures, vital though they are. The role of Her Majesty's Inspectorate of Constabulary (HMIC) is critically important in terms of inspecting forces to ensure that they are delivering effective services. HMIC's principal means of underpinning this work has been its new baseline assessments, which were published for the first time in June 2004. These assessments set baselines for particular activities against which forces should be performing. Movement from the baseline – either improvement or deterioration – is then identified. This allows HMIC's subsequent involvement to be focused on the areas within a force that need most work.

vi. These changes mean that performance in the police is now measured for both quantity and quality in a far more sophisticated way than even three years ago. Combining the Police Standards Unit's objective, quantitative view of performance with HMIC's qualitative assessments provides definitive, up-to-date appraisal of how a force is serving the public in comparison to other forces.

Appendix III: Serious Organised Crime Agency

i. Organised crime reaches into every community, ruining lives, driving other crime and instilling fear. It manifests itself most graphically in drug addiction, in sexual exploitation and in gun crime. It is also big business. Trafficking in people and drugs, counterfeiting and financial crime have a UK turnover of many billions of pounds annually.

ii. Organised crime groups are also highly sophisticated, working in tight knit structures and prepared to use ruthless measures to achieve their objectives. Their illicit activities are underpinned by sophisticated money laundering operations, which turn the proceeds of crime into bankable profits. Groups operate across international frontiers, their influence corrupting government and law agencies in many states world wide, which desperately need good and honest government as a foundation for prosperity, order and security.

iii. A successful approach to organised crime is therefore inseparable from our wider effort to improve the overall effectiveness of policing in this country and to make vulnerable communities and law-abiding citizens safer. It requires that our police forces, our prosecutors, our intelligence services and our national enforcement agencies work together still more closely. Accordingly, having undertaken an extensive review of the case for a single agency against organised crime, the Home Secretary announced his intention to create a Serious Organised Crime Agency in February 2004. The findings were set out in the White Paper "One Step Ahead", launched on 29 March 2004[6].

iv. The Government intends the new Agency to be up and running by April 2006 bringing together the National Crime Squad, the National Criminal Intelligence Service, HM Customs and Excise investigative and intelligence work on serious drug trafficking and recovering related assets, and the Immigration Service's work on organised immigration crime. The new organisation will be driven by intelligence and focused on reducing the enormous harm caused by organised crime to individuals, to communities and to the well being of the country.

v. The Agency will be a wholly new body, operating in new ways and driven by the intelligence assessment of what will be most effective in terms of harm reduction. By removing the organisational boundaries that divide the present agencies, the Government expects the Agency to deliver significantly enhanced operational effectiveness with the objective of making the UK one of the least attractive locations in the world for organised crime to operate.

vi. The Agency will fight, at a national and international level, the full range of organised crime activities including:

- Serious drug trafficking and the recovery of related criminal assets

- People smuggling/trafficking

- Firearms trafficking

- Money laundering of the proceeds of acquisitive crime

- Extortion

- Cyber crime

- Counterfeiting

---

[6] One Step Ahead: a 21st Century Strategy to Defeat Organised Crime (March 2004, Cm 6167)

vii. The Agency will continue to work closely with the police service on intelligence and operations to ensure that there is an effective link between its efforts to combat organised crime at national level and the work being done by police forces at local level.

viii. The Government plans to legislate at the earliest available opportunity to create the new Agency. The legislation will set out the constitutional and governance arrangements of the new Agency, provide it and its staff with necessary powers, and set out its accountability to Ministers. In the interim period, before the Agency comes formally into existence, Sir Stephen Lander (former Director General of the Security Service) and William Hughes (former Director General of the National Crime Squad) have already been appointed as Chairman and Director General designate respectively. They took up their posts in September 2004 and will play crucial roles in setting the direction and making the key early decisions in the lead-in to the formal establishment of the Agency and in planning and delivering an orderly transition.

Appendix IV: Crime and Disorder Act 1998

Background

i. If we are to be successful in the longer term in tackling the social, economic and environmental drivers of crime and disorder, collaborative, co-ordinated, community based action must take place within an enabling legislative framework, supported by a strong relationship between central and local government. The Crime and Disorder Act 1998 recognised the central importance of collaboration. It placed a duty on local authorities and the police to work in partnership and with a wide range of other agencies from the public, private, voluntary and community sectors to develop and implement strategies to reduce crime and disorder at local level. Following the Police Reform Act 2002, this duty was extended to police authorities, fire authorities, Primary Care Trusts (in England) and health authorities (in Wales). Similarly, the remit of partnerships was broadened to include action to address the misuse of drugs.

ii. There are now 354 Crime and Disorder Reduction Partnerships in England and 22 Community Safety Partnerships in Wales. Some work well, implementing robust multi-agency strategies shaped by the needs and concerns of local people, contributing to sustained reductions in crime and tangible improvements in local quality of life. However, some CDRPs are demonstrably less effective than others. For example, partnerships sometimes struggle to maintain a full contribution from key agencies. Lack of clarity about roles and responsibilities and blurred lines of accountability can lead to some agencies abrogating their responsibility for crime reduction. Furthermore, under present arrangements, CDRPs are neither fully visible nor properly accountable to the communities they serve, nor are they firmly embedded in the local democratic framework. These issues lie at the heart of the Government's reform programme.

iii. The Government's overriding aim is to make CDRPs the most effective possible vehicle for tackling crime, anti-social behaviour and substance misuse in their communities. In support of this, we intend to review formally the partnership provisions of the Crime and Disorder Act 1998 (as amended by the Police Reform Act 2002). The review will consider which aspects of existing legislation are most effective and which have been less successful and why. It will recommend legislative and other changes to enable local agencies to work together more effectively with local people to combat crime, anti-social behaviour and drug misuse in their communities.

Scope

iv. The review will consider the provisions outlined in sections 5-7, 17 and 115 of the Crime and Disorder Act 1998, along with sections 97 and 98 of the Police Reform Act 2002. More specifically, it will explore:

- **Role** – the role of CDRPs, including their responsibility for determining strategic priorities for local community safety and delivering on them;

- **Accountability** – how the work of partnerships is scrutinised and how CDRPs can be held to account through the local democratic process. This will include examining the potential for using scrutiny committees and other governance mechanisms for this purpose;

- **Inspection** – making sure individual agencies' inspection regimes take account of their contribution to partnership working; and identifying ways of assessing partnership performance through joint inspection of CDRPs;

- **Community engagement** – how partnerships best engage in ongoing dialogue with all sections of the communities they serve, how this informs CDRP decision-making and how CDRPs demonstrate responsiveness to the needs and concerns of local people;

- **CDRP membership** – how to ensure the right people are working together at the right level to combat crime, disorder and the misuse of drugs, with clearly identified roles and responsibilities, as well as consequences for poor levels of participation. We will consider the role of elected councillors as well as potential new responsible authorities;

- **Mainstreaming (section 17)** – how community safety can be most effectively mainstreamed into key partners' business, including systematic mechanisms for assessing and rewarding compliance, and specific consequences of non-compliance. The review will also assess whether section 17 currently covers the right agencies and bodies and will recommend extending its scope where appropriate;

- **Two-tier working** – how best to manage delivery in areas with two tiers of local government, given that CDRPs are sited at district level but many of the functions and services crucial to sustained crime reduction are the responsibility of the county council. We will also consider the implications for, and potential role of, elected regional assemblies in respect of partnership working to tackle crime;

- **CDRP mergers** – whether to extend the circumstances in which small adjoining CDRPs should be merged in order to achieve greater efficiency;

- **Boundaries** – the effect of partner agencies' different boundaries on partnership work and how best to remove the barriers these differences in boundaries sometimes cause;

- **Drugs and alcohol** – reinforcing the new joint approach to tackling local crime and disorder problems in conjunction with issues around the misuse of drugs and alcohol. This will include assessing how far the integration of CDRPs and Drug Action Teams has taken place to reflect this;

- **Other local agencies** – how the work of CDRPs feeds into and connects with that of other local partnerships, such as Local Strategic Partnerships, Local Criminal Justice Boards, Youth Offending Teams and the wider Criminal Justice System;

- **Funding** – to review the arrangements by which CDRPs fund and commission services from the police and other delivery partners in support of local priorities; and

- **Data sharing** – how best to encourage better data and information sharing between agencies for the purposes of crime reduction.

The review will be conducted between November 2004 and January 2005 with the direct involvement of key stakeholders. It will link with wider developments in public sector reform, most notably police and local government reform, and be underpinned by an unambiguous focus on raising partnership performance through improving accountability and visibility.

Appendix V: Police Authority Membership

i. The proposals for changes to the membership of police authorities set out in Chapter Five will affect the means by which independent and, in some areas, councillor members of police authorities are appointed. This Appendix sets out the approach for both.

Independent members

ii. The Government's proposal is that there should be an appointment panel for independent members for each police force area, consisting of five members, rather than the three members of the present selection panels. Of the five members of the new appointment panel, three should be drawn from the police authority, and two should be independent of the police authority, one being appointed by the Home Secretary and the other being an independent assessor trained and accredited by the Office of the Commissioner for Public Appointments or other similar body.

iii. The appointments process should, throughout, be conducted in line with the spirit of the Commissioner for Public Appointments' Code of Practice and the Cabinet Office Best Practice Guide for making public appointments. Appointments should be made on merit and ability, judged against a competency-based framework of criteria, to complement the existing range of skills, knowledge and experience of police authority members. There should also be set criteria about diversity (race, gender, age, skills, for example) and a requirement to ensure proper engagement and out-reach to get the right people onto the authority. Independent members selected by the appointment panel should be restricted to two terms (eight years) of membership.

iv. The Home Secretary's current role of halving the size of the long-list of candidates in each police authority area before returning the list back to police authorities should end. However, the Government believes that the Home Secretary should retain some fall-back powers through a power of veto over the appointment of candidates who have been sifted and interviewed by the appointments panel and through the appointment of one member of the appointments panel.

v. The sift and interview record sheets of the chosen candidates should be sent to the Home Office and be available to Ministers after interview, together with a report signed by all members of the panel, explaining the process and the reasons for the proposed appointment or appointments. In the event that the Home Secretary was dissatisfied with any name on the proposed list of appointments, the next name in order of preference should be chosen and reasons given for the Home Secretary's veto being applied (except in the case of a breach of confidentiality, ongoing police or other enquiries, or reasons of national security). In accordance with good practice, there should be a proper audit trail covering any such decisions. The Government believes that this change should result in much less frustration among potential independent members who go through the first stage of the application process, only to be rejected according to unclear criteria before the final appointments process begins.

Illustrative examples of effect of proposals on police authority councillor membership

vi. Where police force areas include unitary councils only (seven English forces in total – Cleveland, Greater Manchester, Humberside, Merseyside, South Yorkshire, West Midlands and West Yorkshire and all four Welsh forces – Gwent, South Wales, Dyfed-Powys and North Wales), the Government proposes that the councillor with cabinet responsibility for community safety should be appointed to the police authority. Any remaining councillor places would be filled on a basis designed to ensure that the overall councillor membership of the police authority reflected political balance of the force area as a whole and that there was a geographical spread of councillor members. All corners of the force area with their potentially very different communities and issues should be represented on the police authority. The presumption would be that no police authority would have fewer than 17 members and no authority would have more than 21 members. The current balance where councillor members had a majority on the police authority of 50% plus one would also be maintained.

Unitary councils

vii. Where a force area included only unitary councils, the presumption would be that each unitary council's councillor with cabinet responsibility for community safety would be a member of the police authority. For any remaining councillor places, two of the deciding criteria should be designed to ensure that the overall councillor membership of the police authority should reflect, wherever possible, the political balance of the force area as a whole and ensure that there was a geographical spread of councillor members.

viii. *Example 1 – Greater Manchester Police* force area covers the metropolitan districts of Bolton, Bury, Manchester, Oldham, Rochdale, Salford, Stockport, Tameside, Trafford and Wigan. These ten councils would all be represented on the Greater Manchester Police Authority by their cabinet members with responsibility for community safety. To maintain the 50% plus one majority of councillor members on the police authority, there would be nine independent members, making 19 in total.

ix. *Example 2 – South Yorkshire Police* force area covers the metropolitan districts of Barnsley, Doncaster, Rotherham and Sheffield. These four councils would be represented on the South Yorkshire Police Authority by their cabinet members with responsibility for community safety plus five other councillors chosen to reflect the overall political balance and ensure geographical spread. Thus, the police authority would have nine councillor members and eight independent members, making a total membership of 17 and maintaining the 50% plus one councillor majority.

x. *Example 3 – Dyfed-Powys Police* force area covers the counties of Ceredigion, Carmarthenshire, Pembrokeshire and Powys. These four councils would be represented on the Dyfed-Powys Police Authority by their cabinet members with responsibility for community safety, plus five other councillors chosen to reflect the overall political balance and ensure geographical spread. Thus the police authority would have nine councillor members and eight independent members, making a total membership of 17 and maintaining the 50% plus one councillor majority.

Combination of county, unitary and district councils

xi. The Government recognises the complexity of two-tier local government arrangements. This being the case, we will discuss further with stakeholders proposals for change in these areas. We have developed one option for consideration on councillor police authority membership in areas with a combination of county, unitary and district councils, which we set out below.

xii. Where a force area included both unitary and two-tier councils, the presumption would be that unitary councils would be represented by their councillor with cabinet responsibility for community safety thus ensuring that the biggest population centres in the force area were guaranteed representation on the police authority. Assuming an authority with 17 members, councillors would still have nine places. Five of these would go to the unitary and county councils and four to the district councils. Two of the deciding criteria for filling these four places would be that the overall councillor membership of the authority should reflect the political balance of the force area as a whole and that there was a geographical spread of councillor members. This might mean district councillors on police authorities would have to cover more than one district but part of the selection process should be to establish that they are able and willing to do so.

xiii. *Example 3 – Hertfordshire Constabulary* force area covers the county of Hertfordshire and ten district councils (North Hertfordshire, East Hertfordshire, Stevenage, Broxbourne, Welwyn/Hatfield, St Albans, Dacorum, Three Rivers, Watford and Hertsmere). To make the split between county and district councillors more straightforward, it might be sensible to give the authority 11 councillor places and ten independents, making its total membership 21. Thus, the county council would be represented by the councillor with cabinet responsibility for community safety plus five other councillors chosen to reflect the political balance of the county council and to ensure geographical spread. The remaining five councillor places would be allocated to councillors from the district councils covering two districts each within the force area.

xiv. *Example 4 – Leicestershire Constabulary* force area covers the county of Leicestershire and the unitary councils of Leicester and Rutland, plus seven districts (North West Leicestershire, Charnwood, Melton, Hinckley and Bosworth,

Blaby, Oadby and Wigton and Harborough). Given the population spread, it might be appropriate to allocate two councillor places on the police authority to both Leicestershire County Council and Leicester Council and one to Rutland to give the county and unitary areas the five members this approach proposes. Again, the councillor with cabinet responsibility for community safety on these three councils would be the police authority member with the second Leicestershire and Leicester councillor places and the four district councillor places selected with regard to political balance and geographic spread. The split between the seven district councils is not straightforward and might have to be decided on population spread, for example. The overall authority size would be 17 members.

xv. *Example 5 – Bedfordshire Police* force area covers the county of Bedfordshire and the unitary council of Luton plus three district councils (Bedford, Mid Bedfordshire and South Bedfordshire). The five councillor members from the county and unitary councils might comprise the community safety cabinet member from Bedfordshire County Council plus two other councillors and the community safety cabinet member from Luton Council plus one other councillor. The additional councillors and the four district councillors would also be chosen with regard to political balance and geographical spread with, perhaps, two for Bedford and one each for Mid and South Bedfordshire. Again, the overall authority size would be 17 members.

xvi. **We are interested in hearing views on the relative strengths of this option for councillor membership of police authorities or hearing about other possible formulations and models.**

Appendix VI: The Tripartite Relationship

Government and Home Secretary

- The Home Secretary has overall responsibility for ensuring the delivery of an efficient and effective police service in England and Wales.

- The national framework set by the Home Secretary includes the key priorities for policing and the means by which achievement of these priorities will be measured. These are set out in the National Policing Plan, presented to Parliament on an annual basis.

- Performance monitoring, evaluation and management are co-ordinated at national level by the Police Standards Unit acting on behalf of the Home Secretary with support, engagement and, ultimately, intervention, when necessary, where performance is failing.

- Certain policing approaches (e.g. the National Intelligence Model NIM) and technology (e.g. Airwave) are prescribed nationally to ensure consistency and economies of scale.

- The Home Secretary has national responsibility for counter-terrorism and the Security Service and consequent oversight of force level input to the national counter-terrorist effort.

- The Home Secretary and the Deputy Prime Minister work together to ensure there is adequate provision in the local government settlement for the central police grant.

- Pay and conditions, pensions and regulations are set nationally to ensure fairness and consistency.

Chief Officers

- Chief officers have operational responsibility for effective and efficient policing in their force area.

- Deployment of officers and staff and efficient resource usage are the responsibility of chief officers.

- Performance monitoring and evaluation against national and local performance indicators are the responsibility of chief officers.

- Reductions in crime, anti-social behaviour and disorder as well as improvement in public satisfaction and detections are the responsibility of chief officers.

- Chief officers should ensure that their forces are able to deal effectively and efficiently with national and cross-border crime, including counter-terrorism.

- Chief officers are responsible for ensuring that their force is working in partnership with the communities it serves and communicates effectively with local citizens. This includes the provision of information on local policing issues and openness to local people's views.

- Partnership working, both across the criminal justice service and with other local agencies, is the responsibility of chief officers.

Police Authorities

- Police authorities are responsible for ensuring that an effective and efficient police service is in place in their area.

- The police authority selects the chief officer for the force area. They also have a minority role in recruitment and selection of the deputy chief and the rest of the force's chief officer team (ACCs etc.)

- Police authorities set the personal performance objectives and conduct the performance appraisal of the chief officer.

- Police authorities decide the locally raised precept for policing (via the council tax) and allocate the budget to chief officers.

- Police authorities should hold the chief officer to account for how the key priorities in the National Policing Plan are addressed in their force area and what arrangements are in place for identifying local priorities.

- Police authorities should also hold the chief officer to account for regular engagement and publication of information on force performance.

- Police authorities ensure that performance management arrangements are in place that are transparent and capable of interrogation. They should know whether their chief is reducing crime, anti-social behaviour and disorder and making the best use of the resources available.

- Police authorities are responsible for ensuring that public accountability arrangements are in place at Basic Command Unit and neighbourhood level that enable local people to have a say in how they are policed and identify local priorities within the national framework.

Appendix VII: Glossary of Terms

Anti-Social Behaviour Orders (ASBOs):
ASBOs protect the public from behaviour that causes or is likely to cause harassment, alarm or distress. An order contains certain conditions prohibiting the offender from specific anti-social acts or entering defined areas and is effective for a minimum of two years.

Assets Recovery Agency (ARA): The Agency was established under the Proceeds of Crime Act 2002 to co-ordinate activity across the UK in recovering unlawfully obtained assets from those with no right to hold them. The agency became operational in February 2003.

Association of Chief Police Officers (ACPO):
ACPO exists to promote leadership excellence by the chief officers of the police service, to assist in setting the policing agenda by providing professional opinion on key issues identified to the Government, appropriate organisations and individuals and to be the corporate voice of the service.

Association of Police Authorities (APA):
The APA was set up in 1997 to represent police authorities in England, Wales and Northern Ireland nationally and to strengthen and support the role of police authorities locally. The APA represents police authorities in consultation on police matters and supports police authorities in their work by providing training, publications and research.

Basic Command Unit (BCU): BCUs are the main operating unit of police forces. Typically, a force will divide its territorial area into between three to ten BCUs (in the Metropolitan Police they are called "boroughs" and there are thirty-two) covering areas such as a town or district. They are usually commanded by a superintendent or chief superintendent and consist of several hundred police officers and staff. The officer in charge of a BCU will be tasked by his or her chief constable with policing that locality and day to day decisions will be made as close to communities as possible.

British Association of Women Police (BAWP): BAWP was formed in order to fill a gap within the police service, with its main objectives to enhance the role and understanding of the specific needs of the women who are employed therein.

CENTREX: The Central Police Training and Development Authority known as Centex, defines, develops and promotes excellence. It does so by providing a centre of policing excellence and support, and by creating and implementing the means to develop competence through policing careers.

Commission for Racial Equality (CRE): The CRE is a publicly funded, non-governmental body set up under the Race Relations Act 1976 to tackle racial discrimination and promote racial equality. It works in both the public and private sectors to encourage fair treatment and to promote equal opportunities for everyone, regardless of their race, colour, nationality, or ethnic origin.

Community support officer (CSO): CSOs are police authority employed staff who can perform a high visibility, patrolling role. They complement the work of police officers by focusing predominantly on lower level crime, disorder and anti-social behaviour, providing reassurance to the communities they serve.

Connexions: Connexions is for 13-19 year olds, living in England, who want advice on getting on to where they want to be in life. The service is managed locally by Connexions Partnerships, of which there are 47 throughout the country, which bring together all the key youth support services.

Crime and Disorder Reduction Partnership (CDRP): The Crime and Disorder Act 1998 (as amended by the Police Reform Act 2002) sets out the framework for CDRPs, in which 'responsible authorities' are required to work together in partnership to tackle crime, disorder and the misuse of drugs. The responsible authorities consist of all the local authorities in a CDRP area, the police, police authority, fire authority and Primary Care Trust.

Drug Action Team (DAT): DATs are local partnerships charged with responsibility for delivering the National Drug Strategy at a local level, with representatives from the local authority (education, social services, housing) health, probation, the prison service and the voluntary sector. The English DATs are aligned with local authority boundaries, and have, in many areas, integrated their working practices with the local CDRP.

Fixed Penalty Notices (FPN): Fixed penalty notices are issued where there is reason to believe that an individual has committed a criminal offence for which a FPN is available – a "penalty offence". The majority of tickets are issued for motoring offences, but a range of anti-social and nuisance offences have recently been introduced, for which penalty notices for disorder (PNDs) may be issued. The amount of the penalty varies considerably, up to a maximum of £200. Notices may be issued by a number of authorised individuals, including police officers, community support officers and local authority officers.

Gay Police Association: The Gay Police Association works towards equal opportunities for lesbian and gay police service employees, offering advice and support to lesbian and gay police service employees and promoting better relations between the police service and the lesbian and gay community.

Her Majesty's Inspectorate of Constabulary (HMIC): HMIC is an independent inspectorate established over a century ago. It is responsible for promoting the efficiency and effectiveness of policing in England, Wales and Northern Ireland through inspection of police organisations and functions to ensure agreed standards are achieved and maintained, good practice is spread and performance is improved. It also provides professional advice and support to the tripartite partners (Home Secretary, police authorities and forces) and plays an important role in the development of future leaders.

High Potential Development Scheme (HPD): The High Potential Development Scheme is a competency based, structured career framework which can lead to the most senior positions in the police service. It aims to turn potential into performance, whether as a highly effective middle manager in command and leadership roles, or beyond at the strategic leadership level of the police service.

Independent Police Complaints Commission (IPCC): Established under the Police Reform Act 2002 and operational since April 2004, the IPCC replaced the Police Complaints Authority and deals with serious complaints against the police.

Local Authority Overview and Scrutiny Committees: These committees were established in the Local Government Act 2000. Consisting of councillors who are not members of the cabinet or 'executive', scrutiny committees are responsible for developing and reviewing council policy; holding the executive to account for their actions and decisions; assisting with best value reviews; and external scrutiny – scrutinising the work and impact of other agencies on the local community. In addition to these core responsibilities, the Act empowers scrutiny committees to make reports and recommendations on any matter affecting the local area or its inhabitants.

Local Strategic Partnership (LSP): LSPs are local authority-wide, non-statutory partnerships that work together to identify common objectives for the local community. They include representatives from the public, private, business, voluntary and community sectors. LSPs are obligatory in 88 designated neighbourhood renewal areas but have also been formed in many other areas.

Local Criminal Justice Boards (LCJB): The 42 Local Criminal Justice Boards were set up in April 2003 to manage the Criminal Justice System at a local level. They comprise the chief officers of key criminal justice agencies in each area and report to the National Criminal Justice Board. They ensure a joined up approach to reducing crime, bringing more offenders to justice and improving public confidence in the Criminal Justice System.

Local Government Association (LGA): The LGA exists to promote better local government, working with and for member authorities to realise a shared vision of local government that enables local people to shape a distinctive and better future for their locality and its communities. The LGA aims to put local councils at the heart of the drive to improve public services and to work with government to ensure that the policy, legislative and financial context in which they operate, supports that objective.

National Black Police Association (NBPA): This is an umbrella organisation representing the views of 38 Black Police Associations (BPAs) in the UK. The NBPA aims to promote good race relations and equality of opportunity within the police services and the wider community.

National Centre for Policing Excellence (NCPE): The National Centre for Policing Excellence, which forms part of the Central Police Training and Development Authority (Centrex), was launched on 8 April 2002. It is tasked with developing and disseminating best practice.

National Crime Squad (NCS): The National Crime Squad targets criminal organisations committing serious and organised crime which transcends national and international boundaries, typically drug trafficking, money laundering, counterfeit currency, kidnap and extortion. While NCIS gathers intelligence on these issues, NCS deals with the investigation of such crimes.

National Criminal Intelligence Service (NCIS): NCIS provides actionable intelligence to law enforcement agencies at home and abroad in order to combat and prevent serious and organised crime that impacts on the UK.

National Intelligence Model (NIM): NIM is a model for policing that ensures that information is fully researched, developed and analysed to provide intelligence that senior managers can use to provide strategic direction, make tactical resourcing decisions about operational policing and manage risk. NIM is not just about crime and not just about intelligence – it is a model that can be used for most areas of policing. It offers, for the first time, the realisable goal of integrated intelligence in which all forces and law enforcement agencies play a part in a system bigger than themselves.

National Policing Plan: The national strategic framework for policing in England and Wales is set out in the National Policing Plan, which the Government is required to publish annually. The Plan sets out minimum standards against which policing should be delivered locally.

Office of Public Service Reform: To strengthen the Government's ability to improve public services, the Prime Minister established the Office of Public Service Reform in 2001. Based in the Cabinet Office, OPSR is responsible for pushing forward the reform of public services in accordance with the Prime Minister's four principles of reform, in order to improve customers' experiences of those services.

Police Advisory Board (PAB): The Police Advisory Board advises the Home Secretary on general questions affecting the police in England and Wales.

Police Information Technology Organisation (PITO): Working closely with its partners, PITO provides information technology and communication systems to the police service and criminal justice organisations in the UK. It also has a role in getting best value for the police service on the goods and services they buy. This is done through setting up collective procurement arrangements. PITO is a Non-Departmental Public Body funded by the grant-in-aid and charges for the services it provides.

Police Licensing and Accreditation Board (PLAB): The PLAB is a sub-group of the Police Training and Development Board established to secure appropriate accreditation for all policing skills and to ensure that the learning programmes used to develop such skills are of good quality.

Police Negotiating Board (PNB): PNB was set up to negotiate the hours of duty; leave; pay and allowances; the issue, use and return of police clothing, personal equipment and accoutrements; and pensions of United Kingdom police officers, and to make recommendations to the Home Secretary, Secretary of State for Northern Ireland and Scottish Ministers on these matters.

Police Performance Monitors: These are interim, annual publications detailing performance of the 43 Home Office police forces of England and Wales across a set of performance indicators in use while the Policing Performance Assessment Framework is being prepared.

Police staff: Police staff are non sworn employees within the police service who carry out many functions which enable police officers to patrol, tackle crime and disorder and perform all the other tasks that are expected of them.

Police Staff Council (PSC): The PSC is a voluntary negotiation body (unlike the Police Negotiating Board) which negotiates for 50,000 police staff in England and Wales (excluding the Metropolitan Police). The national agreements of the PSC are only binding if police authorities and chief constables agree to incorporate them within the contracts of employment of their employees.

Police Standards Unit (PSU): The Police Standards Unit, within the Home Office, was set up in June 2001 to help deliver the Government's commitment to raise standards and improve operational performance of the police in order to maintain and enhance public satisfaction with policing in their areas. It does this through, for example, performance monitoring and targeted support for police forces and Basic Command Units.

Police Training and Development Board (PTDB): The Police Training and Development Board (PTDB) was established in May 2002 as the key strategic body with national responsibility for bringing about improvements in police training and development. Replacing the Police Training Council, the PTDB is charged by the Home Secretary to oversee the delivery of the Government's strategy to reform the police service in relation to training and development.

Policing Performance Assessment Framework (PPAF): PPAF is intended to be an effective and fair way of measuring, comparing and assessing strategic performance in policing across the full range of policing responsibilities.

Primary Care Trusts (PCT): PCTs control local health care, while 28 new strategic Health Authorities monitor performance and standards. There are 302 PCTs covering all parts of England, which receive budgets directly from the Department of Health.

Professionalising the Investigative Process (PIP): Professionalising the Investigative Process aims to bring policing into the 21st century by examining existing investigation procedures and developing ways to make the process more professional, ethical and effective for both officers and police staff involved in investigations.

Skills for Justice: Skills for Justice is the sector skills council for the justice sector. It is uniquely placed to bring together the component parts within the justice sector to form a coherent whole, to create better networking of information and provide a single focus on skills issues for the justice sector.

Special constables: special constables are members of the public who volunteer four or more hours a week to help their local police force and represent a partnership of the police and community working together. They are different from other volunteer/community groups in that they are trained officers with full police powers.

Stephen Lawrence Steering Group: This steering group oversees implementation of the Stephen Lawrence Inquiry's recommendations, ensuring that the Executive, the Crown Office and the police service comply with these recommendations.

Sure Start: Sure Start is the Government's programme to deliver the best start in life for every child by bringing together early education, childcare, health and family support.

Wardens: Unlike community support officers, neighbourhood wardens do not have any police powers. Rather, they are the eyes and ears of the community, looking to improve the quality of life of an area and help it along the path to regeneration. As well as providing a link between local residents and key agencies such as the local authority and the police, wardens can also help with efforts to promote community safety and tackle environmental problems such as litter, graffiti, dog fouling and housing.

Youth Offending Teams (YOTS): The YOTs are key to the success of the Youth Justice System, assessing the needs of youth offenders and identifying suitable programmes to address those needs in order to prevent re-offending. Each YOT is managed by a YOT manager, and is made up of representatives from the police, Probation Service, social services, health, education, drugs and alcohol misuse and housing officers.

Appendix VIII: How to comment

If you wish to provide us with your views
on this policy paper please either email us at
police.consultation@homeoffice.gsi.gov.uk or
write to us at:

Building Communities, Beating Crime
Police Reform Unit
6th Floor, Open Plan
50 Queen Anne's Gate
London
SW1H 9AT

Comments on the issues raised in this paper are
required by **Tuesday 1st February 2005**.

Regulatory Impact Assessment

A Regulatory Impact Assessment on this policy
paper has been published and is available at
www.policereform.gov.uk.

Printed in the UK for The Stationery Office Limited
on behalf of the Controller of Her Majesty's Stationery Office
ID 174363 11/04